Letters Of A Dissatisfied Woman

The Fine Art of Complaining

Ingrid Stone

Illustrated by Tim Rockins

Published in the UK by The Pen Nib Press
email: pennibpress@outlook.com
www.thepennibpress.com

Letterbox photograph by Ingrid Stone

Illustrations and wallpaper by Tim Rockins
www.timrockins.com

A catalogue record for this book is available from the British Library

ISBN: 978-0-9928011-0-6

Printed and Bound in Great Britain by
CPI Antony Rowe, Chippenham and Eastbourne

"The Queen of Complaints"
-The Daily Mail

A Dissatisfied Woman

Introduction by Ingrid Stone

As an aspiring eight-year old with especially high standards, my grandmother teased that I would grow up to become a lavatory inspector.

I wrote my first complaint letter at the age of eight, when I won an exceedingly soiled doll at a funfair in Torquay. The reason I still have the letter is that the funfair had disappeared when I went to deliver it the following day.

Here is that letter – I might have had some help in writing it, I cannot imagine many eight-year olds would be aware of such terms as "Dear Sirs" (or Madams for that matter.)

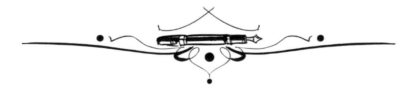

Dear Sirs,

When I was at the Fair I won a prize and it was a doll which was very dirty and i think you should have better prizes than that. My Grandpa tried very hard. to win a prize for Me. and I was disappointed. to get such a dirty doll. Because I wanted a friend for my monkey to play whith But the doll is too dirty. For my monkey who is very fussy.

Will you please tell the people at the Fair. to have clean prizes. In Future, or I will not come to the fair in Torquay any more, but will go somewhere else instead. My Grandma and Grandpa are going to take me to a fair in London and I hope the prizes will be clean and that I may win a Teddy Bear, because in Torquay you don't let people win the Teddy Bears.

I hope you will reply to this letter Quickly.

Ingrid Stone

I am consistently irritated that more people do not complain. They are expert *grumblers*, but rather than make the effort to change anything for the better, they proffer a clipped, and somewhat impotent *tut*, expecting the world at large to interpret the intricacies of that sound (made by a tongue sucking at the base of the front two top teeth).

Because of this Tut, small businesses, local councils, parliamentary candidates, large companies and major corporations will unknowingly continue to displease customers – and at their own expense. As my Grandpa Tony – a successful wine merchant (and something of a *bon viveur*), used to say: *"it's not the customers who complain you should worry about, it's the ones that **don't** complain"*. In other words, all those grumblers and ineffective tut-ters might just not bother to use your products or services again, without telling you – yet tell all their friends, or worse, tweet about it. Grandpa also said: *"it can take a long time to gain a new customer and approximately two seconds to lose them"*. It works both ways. In this economic age, consumers do not want to spend money on products or services that are not up to scratch while companies cannot afford to lose business.

This book is not a guide on how to complain – although I have shared one or two rules, but if it inspires in the slightest, then I am delighted.

Rules Of A Dissatisfied Woman

I feel I would not be doing my duty as a seasoned complainer if I did not impart a few rules.

1. If you are dissatisfied, do not suffer in silence.

2. Do not forget that you have paid good money. Why do you not deserve what you have paid for?

3. Always complain in writing. In that way you have a proper record of the situation.

4. Always complain to the person at the top. You might not get a response from them but at least your complaint will (usually) be treated seriously and handed to someone with proper authority.

5. If you do not follow Rule 4, it is very unlikely you will receive proper compensation for your complaint. Instead, you will find yourself handled in a typical Join The Queue manner by customer relations departments, particularly if you telephone them: a) you will have trouble getting through to them, and b) they will put you on hold for annoyingly long periods of time, only to then cut you off.

6. Be polite. You want to get something out of this, so it is best not to put other people's backs up. A polite and irritated, rather than a rude and angry tone is more likely to achieve a positive outcome to your letter.

7. Be truthful. You can be colourful when writing your letter – mildly dramatic if necessary, but no porkies please. Remember, two wrongs do not make a right.

8. Adopt a learned tone in your letter. The product or experience you are complaining about might have been sloppy, but you are not. It is important the complainee believes you to be exacting and observant, a person of integrity. Use phrases such as *I felt it necessary to put pen to paper* and *I found myself compelled to write*.

9. Remember that by writing a complaint letter, you have nothing to lose and everything to gain.

10. Make *I DESERVE BETTER* your mantra.

Locating Your Inner Complainer

It is there, somewhere. It might not be apparent at first, but I guarantee you that within your person lurks an indignant, seething tyrant just waiting to expose life's little injustices.

- The 60 Minute Rule Write your letter when the grievance has just taken place – ideally within 60 minutes of the moment occurring. In that way, the experience is still fresh and therefore easier to express. The words will not flow quite as fluently after 60 minutes has passed. In the event of not having the means to pen your complaint within these precious 60 minutes, preferably do it by the end of the day.

- Do not be afraid of initially writing down a train of thought, it can be a great way of letting the back story to your complaint unfold naturally, in an unrestrained way. Plus, the beauty of putting something into words means you can always return and edit it later.

- If complaining is anathema to you, give yourself a moment and allow yourself to get worked up (probably best to check with your doctor first if you suffer from dizzy spells or high blood pressure). Visualise the scene. You have been let down. You are an honest, hard-working person. You have paid money. Times are hard. They are not a charity. How dare they?

- Have a little fun where you can – and where appropriate. Having fun is empowering, so transform a bad experience where you have been made to feel helpless – for example, a delayed or cancelled rail journey, and use word-play and light humour in your letter. It can be surprisingly enjoyable. That aside, good communication skills and making your words stand out (without being defensive or aggressive) are key.

- If you really cannot find your inner complainer, imagine you are someone else. It might be someone you know, a celebrity, or a person you admire. Would they stand for the poor service at that overpriced restaurant? The snagged hem on those new jeans? How would they express themselves? Write your letter using their imagined voice. The letter will be from you, so you don't have to tell them – that is, unless you want to - although I would not recommend telling people they were the inspirational voice for your complaint letter.

Over the years, I have complained (and shall continue to complain), and I have received various compensations - from a sackful of pens and pest control fly-papers to business class flights and a free stay at a four-star hotel. I have also complained on behalf of other people and where there is no financial gain to be had.

A Wee Thought For Trolls

This is NOT about "freebies" (a word I loathe and that has been widely used by the international press to describe some of the 'compensations' received from my complaint letters.) It is about standing up for your rights as a consumer and an individual and trying to make things better. I would be a wretched soul indeed if I double-flipped and whooped after getting £0.20 from Mars Confectionary to make up for a poorly-filled packet of Maltesers.

Here are my letters – well, some of them, along with a few of the responses (the ones that I could find), including some rather less successful than others.

Complaint Letter No. 1

Response: A3 Jiffy bag filled with assorted Pilot Pen Co. UK Ltd. pens - including ballpoints, fine-liners, silver decorative pens and fluorescent markers.

Public Relations Department Pilot Pen Co. UK Ltd.*
Hi-tech House
Malton Avenue
Slough
Bucks SL1 4DE

Dear Sir / Madam

As a regular user of Pilot products, it is with great regret that I must put pen (not Pilot, I'm afraid) to paper and return a packet of Ballpoint GIs.

In my quest for the perfect shorthand pen, I thought these looked just the ticket: "A New Adventure in Writing" - attractive, good value and a thickish point (0.7).

These pens were most definitely a "new adventure" - not only that, they were also a new challenge - so much so, I could not get the bloody thing to write properly.

I am fed up with forking out money on pens that do not write, and I am returning these pens to you with their receipt for a refund. You really should give your pens a thorough test before merchandising them - especially when poor sods like myself are seduced by lies on the packet e.g. "smooth feel". These little blighters are the pen equivalents of a Robin Reliant.

Yours faithfully
Ingrid Stone

*These were early days for the Dissatisfied Woman, hence the letter being addressed to a customer services department and not a person at the top of the Pilot Pen Co. UK Ltd.

Complaint Letter No. 2

Response: Postal order to cover purchase costs incurred, and a pledge by SmithKline Beecham Consumer Healthcare to forward the said dental floss sample to their Quality Control Laboratory for analysis.

Customer Issues Department*
SmithKline Beecham Consumer Healthcare
Brentford TW8 9SD

Dear Sir / Madam

I felt it necessary to put pen to paper and highlight the problems I have experienced with your dental floss (please find enclosed).

This dental floss not only feels like string, it is so difficult to get in between the gums that it actually cuts them - if we were living in Dickensian times, this floss could have been used for extracting patients' teeth.

I am very rarely driven to complain, but at the very least, I expect a full refund. After using your floss, my boyfriend and I were nursing our cut, bleeding gums for some time afterwards.

I look forward to hearing from you.

Yours faithfully
Ingrid Stone

These were early days for the Dissatisfied Woman, hence the letter being addressed to a customer services department and not a person at the top of SmithKline Beecham.

By Appointment to H.M. The Queen
Suppliers of Lozenges
SmithKline Beecham Consumer Healthcare
Brentford, Middlesex

By Appointment to H.R.H. The Prince of Wales
Suppliers of Toothpaste
SmithKline Beecham Consumer Healthcare
Brentford, Middlesex

Direct Line:

Fax: Ref: AS/08/AE26935

Dear Ms Stone

Thank you for your letter concerning Aquafresh Dental Floss. We are sorry to hear of the problems you and your boyfriend experienced whilst using our product.

Although it is unlikely that the pack of Aquafresh Dental Floss that you used is in any way defective, we have forwarded the sample you returned to us to our Quality Control Laboratory for analysis. We will contact you again when we have received their report but must advise you that in some cases this may take several weeks.

We should point out that Aquafresh floss is thicker than traditional floss but thinner than dental tape. People whose teeth are more closely spaced may therefore experience some problems in using the floss.

If you or your boyfriend are at all worried about your condition, we recommend that you contact your dentist for medical advice if you have not already done so.

Because you have returned the product to us, I have enclosed a postal order to cover the purchase costs incurred.

We apologise for the discomfort and inconvenience you have been caused. Thank you for bringing this matter to our attention, and please be assured that the matter will be thoroughly investigated.

Sincerely
for **SMITHKLINE BEECHAM CONSUMER HEALTHCARE**

Alison Sutherland BPharm
Medical Information Executive

Enc: PO

SB House, Brentford, Middlesex TW8 9BD. Telephone: 020 8560 5151
SmithKline Beecham p.l.c. Registered in England and Wales No. 2337959. Registered Office: New Horizons Court, Brentford, Middlesex TW8 9EP.

Complaint Letter No. 3

Response: None.*

Andrew Harrison
Chief Executive
easyJet Airline Company Ltd.
easyLand
London Luton Airport
Bedfordshire LU2 9LS

Dear Mr Harrison

I have just returned from Amsterdam, travelling with easyJet, reference EBFPLGX.

Both the inward and outward flights were excellent (I am usually a very nervous passenger), but I felt so strongly about your in-flight 'service' that I had to write.

The cabin crew on both flights were nothing short of disinterested and rude. On the way out, there was a delay because the crew did not know how many passengers they had on the plane. We were sitting on the runway for about thirty minutes, and so I asked one of the crew members (politely, I hope) how long the delay would be. This crew member barely stopped to listen, and when she spoke, she gave me a resentful glare and muttered sulkily *"we leave when we leave"*.

The return journey was not much better, but to top it off, there was the matter of a cheese baguette. I say 'cheese' in the broadest sense of the word, because what was actually in this five-Euros baguette were two of the smallest pieces of cheese I have ever seen. If you want the mathematical dimensions, I would say (without exaggeration), that the two pieces of cheese in question measured 3 x 6 cm, at 0.5 cm thick. About the right size to entrap two slightly peckish mice.

I do understand that easyJet is a no-frills airline, but really the idea of being treated as some kind of nuisance figure by your staff is shocking. Not only that, five Euros for mousetrap leftovers is unforgivable. No wonder our continental friends mock the English attitude to food.

Yours sincerely
Ingrid Stone

*Do not be put off by this lack of response. Mr Harrison Esq. was an exception to my rule.

Complaint Letter No. 4

Response: A delightful reply signed in Parker blue ink.

Chris Webster
Chief Executive
Woburn Safari Park
Woburn Park
Bedfordshire MK17 9QN

Dear Mr Webster

I recently visited Woburn Safari Park with my partner, thinking it would be a fun day out for him as he is currently on crutches and cannot get around too easily.

We had a lovely time, but I have to say that it was somewhat marred by the appalling food served in your 'restaurant'. Passing tables of other diners poking distrustfully at their plates and playing with their food did little to whet the appetite, and when we approached the buffet area, there was a strange, metallic smell. The food looked inedible even at that distance. Hungry as we were, we struggled to find something we actually wanted to eat. We ended up with an overpriced wrap and sandwich, thinking that the safest option - but of course, the bread was stale.

I find it shocking that this sort of food is allowed to be served - the sort of food to be endured rather than enjoyed, especially when it is sold at overblown prices. In fact, if this can be termed a 'restaurant', then perhaps motorway service stations should rename their establishments 'haute cuisine'.

Yours sincerely
Ingrid Stone

WOBURN
Safari Park

Woburn Safari Park Woburn Bedfordshire MK17 9QN
Tel: 01525 290407 Fax: 01525 290489 Email: info@woburnsafari.co.uk www.discoverwoburn.co.uk

Dear Mr Stone,

Thank you for your letter of the 24th April, regarding your meal experience within the Safari Restaurant. I was most concerned to learn of your disappointment and I thank you for bringing it to my attention.

We try very hard to deliver a consistent and high standard of food and service within the restaurant, but it would appear that we fell short of those standards during your visit, for which I sincerely apologise. I have discussed your letter fully with the Catering Manager, who will communicate your disappointment to his staff team and use it to help illustrate the importance of upholding standards.

I very much hope that during your next visit to the Safari Park you will find that our standards match your expectations.

Yours sincerely

Chris Webster
Chief Executive

WOBURN
The Inn at Woburn

WOBURN
Abbey

WOBURN
Golf Club

Make the discovery

Woburn Enterprises Limited, Registered Office: Bedford Office, Woburn, Milton Keynes MK17 9PQ, Registered in England No. 0966094, VAT No. 68 397 4672

Complaint Letter No. 5

Response: One free night's stay in one of the Corus Hotel Hyde Park's executive rooms with breakfast.

Ron Cox
General Manager
Corus Hotel Hyde Park
Lancaster Gate
London W2 3LG

Dear Mr Cox

I stayed at the Corus Hyde Park with my partner on Tuesday, 10th October, while waiting to move into our new flat, and we were delighted by the hotel's beautiful location and lovely-looking reception area.

Unfortunately, that pleasure was short-lived. While we accepted the small size of our room, we had no idea that our night at the Corus Hyde Park would turn out to be one of the worst nights' sleep we had ever had (quite a feat during our stressful house-moving time).

The bathroom switch (which sat outside the bathroom facing the bed) was illuminated at all times, and a bright green light shone directly at the bed - so much so, it was like trying to sleep at the foot of a traffic light. My partner, who is on crutches, and is usually a sound sleeper, was so fed up with it that he hung his jacket over one of his crutches to prop against, and to block out the light. And then there was the mattress.

So apparent were the springs, I can only describe it as being like sleeping on cotton-covered chicken wire. As for the cherry, there was the matter of the heat. Hot, insufferable heat. We gave up on opening the window because the noise from the Bayswater Road was intolerable. So we tried the fan - but then had to switch it off immediately because it sounded like a small fighter aircraft, and with the walls being as thin as they were (we could hear someone in the next room snoring), we did not want to wake up our neighbours.

If we were lucky, my partner and I might have clocked up three hours' sleep between us, but all-in-all, I can only say that my experience of sleeping at the Corus Hyde Park hotel was akin to enduring a night in Orwell's Room 101.

For a four-star hotel at £149 (excluding a very poor and mean-spirited breakfast - the 'continental' breakfast consisted of cash 'n' carry 'value' style croissants and Laughing Cow cheese triangles), I find this shocking.

Yours sincerely
Ingrid Stone

'A Continental Breakfast'

Corus hotel Hyde Park

Lancaster Gate
London
W2 3LG

Tel 0870 609 6161
Fax 020 7724 8666

e-mail londonhydepark@corushotels.com
www.corushotels.com/londonhydepark

Dear Mrs Stone,

Thank you for your letter following your visit to us on the 10th October.

First and foremost, please at least allow me to apologise for giving you cause to write in the first place, certainly not my intention I assure you.

I'm afraid I won't insult you with any silly, bland excuses, but I will put my hands up and agree with some of your sentiments, because that is without doubt one of our smallest rooms which is usually left as a 'last let'. As such, it should never have been let to you.

I would only say, in a somewhat meek defence that it's the first complaint I've received about the green light since they were installed two years ago. Generally they've been well received, by avoiding the often fumbling about in the night looking for the bathroom in a strange room. But I take your comments on the chin, as a gentleman.

What I'd very much like to do, if of course you have a strong enough constitution, is invite you and your husband back as my guests, when I hope you'll see why we're so busy, largely with repeat guests for the past few years. The offer will include a full English breakfast (I note your views on the continental breakfast, so wouldn't be so foolish to go there), and an executive room, so with luck, your last memory might be erased, or at least dulled somewhat.

When you have a date in mind, simply call me on 020 7298 5459 or e-mail me at rcox@corushotels.com. If I'm away, call the hotel number on this letter and ask for Customer Services when Jacqui or Rohan will make the arrangements.

Dates we're currently already full are the first 10 days of November and the first week of December, otherwise, being something of an irrepressible optimist, I look forward to hearing from you and perhaps meeting you both.

Yours sincerely

Ron Cox
General Manger

Registered office: Plaza on Hyde Park Limited, Blakelands House, Yeomans Drive, Blakelands, Milton Keynes MK14 5HG
Registered in England Number 3447012

A member of The MUI Group

A Postscript

That particular complaint letter had an especially happy ending.
My partner and I had a very enjoyable stay in the executive
room (room 1025) offered to us at the Corus Hotel Hyde
Park. I briefly mentioned to the General Manager that we
would be staying there for the anniversary of when we met, and
we arrived to find a huge bouquet of flowers, plus a box of
Belgium chocolates and a bottle of Champagne waiting for us
in our room. And the next morning, following breakfast in
bed, my partner asked me to marry him - albeit over a
Laughing Cow cheese triangle.

Complaint Letter No. 6

Response: Personal shopper experience and £100 to spend on clothes at Debenhams.

Rob Templeman
Chief Executive
Debenhams Plc.
1 Wellbeck Street
London W1G 0AA

Dear Mr Templeman

As a regular customer at your London Oxford Street branch, I thought Debenhams would be the ideal place to find a wedding dress for my forthcoming wedding.

The Debenhams marketing material in the bridal magazines stated what an excellent service your bridal department offered, and your website even goes so far as to call your bridal advisers 'specialist'.

It was planned. Two appointments made for 31st January: in the morning, House Of Fraser, and in the afternoon, Debenhams. My mother came down to London from Oxford, and we were going to make a special day of it.

After an encouraging start at House Of Fraser, we arrived at the Debenhams bridal department feeling optimistic. But this optimism rather wilted before we even started on the gowns. The 'specialist bridal adviser' sat slumped at a reception desk and barely acknowledged us. She was - dare I say it, utterly grumpy. She did not budge from the desk, and when my mother and I asked what we needed to do (the adviser did not offer us any help), her manner was rude and disinterested. Remaining seated, she pointed in the vague direction of the gowns and cubicles, and she positively begrudged our request when we asked if there were any shoes I could borrow to try on with the dresses. Lord knows why we had to book an appointment with the bridal department when it was clearly up to my mother and I to fend for ourselves.

Weddings are meant to be special, but the bridal department at Debenhams is very far removed. The 'specialist bridal adviser' would have been much more in keeping with manning an institution for young offenders. And I remain intrigued as to what the adviser is a 'specialist' in. My mother and I hastily left Debenhams' bridal department, and it was a relief to return to the warm and helpful assistants at House Of Fraser's bridal department.

It is interesting to note that on the House Of Fraser Designer Bridal Room's website there is no mention of 'specialist bridal advisers'. Perhaps it is just taken as read that their assistants will be courteous and helpful.

Yours sincerely
Ingrid Stone

Po Box 16
334-348 Oxford Street
London W1C 1JG
T: 08445 616161
F: 020 7518 7408 / 7683
www.debenhams.com

Dear Ms Stone,

Thank you for your letter dated 15th February 2007, which has been forwarded to me from Rob Templeman's Office.

I apologise most sincerely for the disappointment that you have encounted while using our Bridal service. We are very sensitive to the importance of this occasion, however, in this instance we have not succeeded in providing the desired level of service.

I honestly believe that it was a genuine mistake and that you went into the Wedding Gifts Registry area rather than the Bridal Suite. This does not excuse the unfortunate service you were given.

The Bridal staff we have here at Debenhams, Oxford Street are a very passionate team and I am surprised to learn that you felt the service they have given you was unsatisfactory. This Service is not typical of the normally high standards that we strive to achieve, as I am sure you are aware, being a regular customer.

I do hope that we are still able to assist you, however, given the time frame from your original visit, I am sure you are already sorted for a bridal gown. I would therefore like to offer you, as a gesture of goodwill, a Personal Shopper experience.

Please therefore accept £100 towards an outfit, which the Personal Shopper will be able to help you select. I hope this helps restore Debenhams good image and your faith in us.

If you have any further enquiries, please don't hesitate to contact me on 020-7518-4702 for assistance in booking your personal shopper experience.

Yours sincerely,

Ian Dallow
Senior Store Manager
Oxford Street

Debenhams Retail plc. Registered in England. Company no. 83395. Registered office 1 Welbeck Street, London W1G 0AA.

Complaint Letter No. 7

Response: One free Bikram yoga session.

Harvey Koniak
Bikram Yoga West
260 Kilburn Lane
London W10 4BA

Dear Mr Koniak

I have been enjoying my Bikram yoga practice at Kilburn Lane for the past month, but I feel obliged to write after last night's 7pm class.
There were sixty-two students during the practice, and it was one of the most uncomfortable occasions I have ever experienced. Sixty-two of us were jam-packed into the room, and I could well relate to how a battery chicken might feel. All sixty-two of us overlapped, and with temperatures of around 40 degrees centigrade, it was utterly claustrophobic. The atmosphere in the room was one of restlessness and irritation. I have been suffering from panic attacks the last couple of months, and I left the class half-way through feeling panicky and utterly stressed out. I was not alone - several other students also left the class.

I think it is a disgrace that so many students are invited to take a class at the same time. It is stress-inducing and unhygienic. I also find it to be the antithesis of what yoga should be about, and it is actually incredibly greedy for your organisation to be thinking more about how much money it is taking rather than the welfare of its members.

Yours sincerely
Ingrid Stone

Complaint Letter No. 8

Response: £0.20 token to spend against any purchase of Mars confectionary.

Fiona Dawson
Managing Director
Mars UK
Dundee Road
Slough
Bucks SL1 4JX

Dear Ms Dawson

As a regular consumer of Maltesers, you can imagine my disappointment when I reached for my Fun Size packet of Maltesers, only to find it somewhat short of a Malteser.

I have enclosed the rogue packet of Maltesers as I think this is something your company should investigate. As you can see (and if you cop a feel), you will observe that there are in fact, only three Maltesers in the packet. Products really should not be going on sale in this way.

Many thanks.

Yours sincerely
Ingrid Stone

Complaint Letter No. 9

Response: £25 credit on my mother's BT account.

Sir Michael Rake
Chairman
BT Group Plc
BT Centre
81 Newgate Street
London EC1A 4AJ

Dear Sir Michael

I have just contacted BT regarding my mother's faulty telephone line, and I felt compelled to write after experiencing something of a farce.

I spent a none-too-meagre amount of time on the telephone with your call centre, and the reason the call took so long was because neither I, nor your staff could convey our meaning to one another due to the appalling line. Irritating to say the least, not to mention - ironic. At one point I was so frustrated with the bad connection that when your staff asked me for a contact number, I could not resist asking if they would be calling from overseas and so would require a +44 prefix. They said they were based in India.

I am actually appalled by this system, which seeing as you are a telecoms company is something of a joke. As it is, I am a busy, working woman and my

mother relies on her telephone for both business and
for keeping in regular contact with her elderly mother
- needless to say, the irony was not appreciated.

I look forward to hearing from you.

Yours sincerely
Ingrid Stone

Sir Michael Rake
Chairman

BT Centre
Room B3AX
81 Newgate Street
London EC1A 7AJ
United Kingdom

Tel +44 (0)20 7356 6666
Fax +44 (0)20 7356 6679
Email cceo@bt.com
BT Centre
Tel +44 (0)20 7356 5000

Dear Mr Slane

I am replying to your letter of 4 December about your mother's faulty telephone line.

As a service industry, we are acutely aware that all our customers should receive a high standard of service at all times; this is a commercial imperative and we are committed to addressing areas of concern. In relation to this, I regret the terrible problems you and your mother experienced in your recent dealings with us. I fully accept that this has been a frustrating experience for you both. In view of this, I felt it important to write to you and offer my personal apology for the inconvenience we have caused you.

Following receipt of your letter, Vinod Badiani of my office spoke with you to offer his apology and to discuss your concern. As Vinod explained, normally the call quality on communication links to our offshore sites is good. However, we have highlighted your correspondence to our senior managers and asked them to take preventative action.

I am glad that the fault on your mother's line is cleared. I realise that compensation is not at the heart of your complaint, but Vinod felt it important to make amends for your poor experience. Accordingly, he has credited your mother's next account with £25.00.

In closing, let me say that what happened here is unfortunate and not typical of the level of service that we provide day in day out to the vast majority of our customers. Please accept my own apology for the inconvenience and undue worry we have caused you and your mother. I hope my personal response and our action assures you that we have taken your complaint seriously. Please do not hesitate to call Vinod on telephone number 020 7356 6666 (or by e-mail at cceo@bt.com) if you have any further enquiries.

Yours sincerely

SIR MICHAEL RAKE

BT Group plc
Registered Office:
81 Newgate Street, London EC1A 7AJ
Registered in England no. 4190816

www.bt.com

Complaint Letter No. 10

By email to Express Herbs

Dear Sir / Madam

I receive emails daily (sometimes bi-daily) from your company about the benefits of enlarging my penis. As a fully-fledged woman in my mid-thirties, I have never - and will never be the possessor of a penis - let alone feel the need to increase any of my appendages by one to three inches.

Please remove me from your mailing list.

Many thanks.

Yours faithfully
Ingrid Stone

Complaint Letter No. 11

Response: Six complimentary return British Airways Club
Europe tickets.

Willie Walsh
Chief Executive
British Airways Plc
Waterside
PO Box 365
Harmondsworth
UB7 0GB

Dear Mr Walsh

No doubt you will have been inundated with
correspondence of late.

I have just returned from a television market in
Cannes, and I write on behalf of myself and my five
colleagues who I travelled with to Nice on Sunday,
6th April. None of us could have foreseen the
subsequent fiasco of the day's events.

We were due to fly out on the BA348 at 15:25 and
according to the check-in desk, there were no delays
expected. After a hurried lunch (somewhat ironically
we did not think we had enough time for a sit-down
meal), the departure board informed us that the flight
was delayed to 19:00. The first blow, although
comparatively minor to what was yet to come.

When I asked your staff in the business lounge for an explanation "only one runway working in Lisbon", "air-crew rotation" and "the weather" were blamed by turns. Apparently there was also not enough provision for de-icing the aircraft. With a mere five to ten millimetres of snow - and most of that melted by midday, our friends in colder climes (where they really do have extremities of weather to contend with) must think this a joke. And with the British propensity to blame the weather for all manner of things, I cannot believe British Airways does not have the foresight to have a back-up crew.

After four hours, my colleagues and I were directed to the gate where we continued to wait patiently until 19:45, when a voice on the Tannoy imparted the bad news of our flight being cancelled. Mayhem ensued. A heart palpitation-inducing cocktail of forty-five minutes until the next flight at 20:30, having to reclaim our baggage and re-check in - not to mention the fight to obtain a standby ticket amid everyone else on the cancelled flight all keen to attend the television market in Cannes.

There was a touch of Dante's Inferno about the baggage hall. Stifling heat, and there was the anarchic dumping of baggage from two other cancelled flights - not on a conveyor belt, I hasten to add, but on the floor. It took us a while to realise that our baggage was still being unloaded and so there was the disturbing prospect of rummaging through floor-strewn suitcases which all looked the same. And of course, time was running out.

My luggage was the last off the conveyor belt, and after a gut-crippling sprint with my suitcase, I rejoined my colleagues and the other passengers from the cancelled flight in the cattle market that was the check-in desk. Lucky for us, we managed to obtain the final six standby tickets. But all the while was the nagging doubt that this flight could well be cancelled too. As it happens, the flight was not cancelled - but there was the matter of crew, plane and captain. This second flight was delayed until midnight because the crew, plane and finally the captain, went missing in succession.

Eventually (and having lost all confidence in British Airways) we landed in Nice - and one would have thought the problems would end there.
Unfortunately, due to our extremely late arrival, the taxis booked to take us to our hotels had given up and we had to wait another two hours for a cab. Once in Cannes, there followed another bartering session, this time with the hotel reception at 4 am - who, because of the tardy check-in, wanted to release our hotel rooms. In fact, when I eventually got to my hotel room, there was a stranger sleeping in my bed.

This is nothing short of appalling. I feel so disturbed by what happened I cannot find the words. I expect a full refund for all our flights at the very least.

Yours sincerely
Ingrid Stone

Willie Walsh
Chief Executive

BRITISH AIRWAYS

Ref 6550404

Waterside (HBB3)
PO Box 365 Harmondsworth UB7 0GB UK
United Kingdom Tel 0870 850 9850
Outside United Kingdom Tel +44 (0)191 490 7901
Fax +44 (0)20 8759 9597

Dear Ms Stone

Thank you for your letter of 11 April 2008.

The time you have taken to write to me in such detail demonstrates just how strongly you feel about the way you were treated on your journey to Nice. Clearly, you had a frustrating and tiring start to your journey and I can make no excuse for the poor impression we have left you and your colleagues with. Please accept my sincere apologies.

I fully understand your disappointment at being told your flight was cancelled – this was certainly not a good start to such an important trip. The initial delay was due to bad weather. The resulting disruptions meant many of our cabin crew and flight crew were out of position. This left us with no alternative but to cancel your flight. To have to collect your baggage and return to check-in must have been extremely frustrating. Arriving in Nice so late to find your taxi had not waited must have felt like the final straw. I am sorry for the distress this obviously caused you.

You are a valuable customer and I recognise we have let you, and your colleagues, down. With this in mind, I would like to offer each of you a complimentary ticket in our Club Europe cabin. My Executive Assistant, Kate Mundy, will send you details of how to book these.

Customer satisfaction is my absolute priority and I am committed to getting all aspects of our service right. I very much hope we are able to restore your confidence in us – and soon.

Yours sincerely

Willie Walsh

28

Complaint Letter No. 12

Response: A pledge by Time Out's editorial staff to look into the issues raised by my letter.

Will Tizard
Editor
Time Out Guides Ltd.
Universal House
251 Tottenham Court Road
London W1T 7AB

Dear Mr Tizard

My husband and I spent a very enjoyable weekend in Prague last month – a final trip abroad for a while as I am pregnant with my first baby, and we armed ourselves with a copy of the 2009 edition of 'Time Out: Prague'.

The guide was most helpful - in particular with its restaurant recommendations, and being in Prague for only a couple of days, we decided to follow Time Out's suggested itinerary "Prague in 48 Hours".

This suggested itinerary is very good, but there are a couple of aspects that need to be clarified in your guide as they are slightly misleading.

The first is that there is no mention of one needing to take transport in order to visit all the sights in the itinerary, and because of this, my husband and I (who are both relatively fit) decided to walk. But being unfamiliar with the area, we had no concept of where the various places were in relation to each other and rather exhausted ourselves trying to cram in everything on foot – which we were unable to manage. Indeed, one would need superhuman strength to visit everything on your list in this way.

The second aspect in your guide that needs further explanation is the lovely Church Of Our Lady Of The Snows. The guide states: "In the church's side chapel (accessible via a door on the right in the rear), you can gawp at the trio of gruesome crucifixes". Following these instructions, my husband and I found ourselves in quite an embarrassing situation. As suggested, we took the "door on the right in the rear", and not only did we not find the church's side chapel - or the aforementioned crucifixes, we discovered that we were - in fact, in the priest's private quarters and shortly after making that discovery, were given a sharp reprimand by the priest residing there.

I really do think it important to clarify these points in your guide. As mentioned, I am currently pregnant – and would have taken transport to visit some of the further-out sights in your itinerary had we known. And equally, the church details should be updated so that future visitors do not find themselves in an awkward position with the priest.

I look forward to hearing from you.

Yours sincerely
Ingrid Stone

The Response (by email)

Dear Ingrid,

Thanks so much for taking the time to send us your feedback on our Prague Guide.

Your comments on the itinerary and the Church of Our Lady of the Snows are very useful. I've sent your letter to Will Tizard, the editor.

Thanks again, and best wishes,
Holly

Holly Pick
Editorial Manager
Time Out Guides
Universal House,
251 Tottenham Court Road,
London, W1T 7AB

Complaint Letter No. 13

Response: Apple was marvellous - I did not have to do a thing. They made certain that the computer was seen immediately and given a priority repair (which they booked in themselves). The repair was free of charge.

Steve Jobs
CEO Apple
Apple Inc.
1 Infinite Loop
MS 301-41R
Cupertino, CA 95014
USA

Dear Mr Jobs

After having had such a good experience with my Apple iBook, I had no hesitation in purchasing the Apple MacBook.

I have to report however, that I am appalled with the build of my computer. I do not know how, but part of the casing has split – and as you can see in the attached photograph, the split casing lifts up all too easily and as a result, it has become difficult to use the computer without it catching on my sleeve. When this happens, the plastic twangs like a ruler caught in a desk, and sooner or later, the plastic is going to snap off completely, leaving a gap in the computer base.

I only purchased this computer three-and-a-half years ago and having forked out a fair bit of money to pay for it, I think it is quite appalling
that this has happened – particularly as Apple prides itself on its strong reputation as a leader in product design.

I would be most grateful if you would look into this issue for me.

I look forward to hearing from you.

Yours sincerely
Ingrid Stone

The Response (by email)

From: Maria Deffense
To: Stone, Ingrid
Subject: Apple Case: 154141439

Dear Mrs. Stone,

Thank you for your letter sent to Apple. Your correspondence concerns an issue that we feel would be best handled in a phone conversation.

Unfortunately, I was unable to contact you on your phone number _____. If you have not yet resolved the issue, please contact me at _____ext ____, Monday through Friday, between 9.00 a.m. and 5.30 p.m. GMT time, or you may send me an email including your telephone number and a preferred time of contact.

I look forward to speaking with you.

Kind regards,
Maria Deffense
Executive Relations EMEA
Apple Sales International
Hollyhill Industrial Estate
Cork, Ireland

Directors: Cathy Kearney (Irish), Gary Wipfler, Peter Oppenheimer & Timothy Cook (United States of America)

Complaint Letter No. 14

Response: Case of 6 x 125g tins Food Thoughts cocoa.

Simon Dunn
Managing Director
Product Chain Ltd
Unit 5
Beech Court
Wokingham Road
Hurst
Berkshire RG10 0RQ

Dear Mr Dunn

I purchased the enclosed jar of Food Thoughts "The Finest Fairtrade" Cocoa with the idea of making Nigella Lawson's chocolate orange cake recipe, which requires a large amount of cocoa in its mixture.

It was lucky I sampled the cocoa before making the cake. In order to make a mug of cocoa (which I was looking forward to), I did as the instructions suggested, and I can only describe the ensuing result as tasting like bad breath. Had I not sampled the cocoa, I can only imagine that an entire cake would taste like a dentist's waiting room where the patients are suffering from collective halitosis. I would have been very embarrassed to serve such a cake to guests.

This is disappointing, as I like to support Fairtrade products wherever I can, but unfortunately I must return your product for a full refund.

I look forward to hearing from you.

Yours sincerely
Ingrid Stone

NORTHERN TEA MERCHANTS

Incorporating Classic Coffees

Telephone: (01246) 232600 (Orders)
(01246) 233660 (Sales)
(01246) 233243 (Enquiries)
(01246) 278625 (Accounts)
Facsimile: (01246) 555991
E-mail: enquiries@northern-tea.com

TEA BAG MANUFACTURERS,
COFFEE ROASTERS,
PACKERS OF TEAS, COFFEES
AND VENDING PRODUCTS

Crown House
193 Chatsworth Road
Chesterfield
Derbyshire S40 2BA

WITHOUT PREJUDICE

RE: COMPLAINT 07

Dear Mrs Stone

I write to acknowledge receipt of your complaint, which arrived yesterday afternoon by email, sent on by Mr Dunn at Product Chain. We are the importers and packers of the Food Thoughts Finest Fairtrade Cocoa and I will personally deal with your letter in accordance with our complaints policy as set out in our quality manual.

I am most disappointed to hear of your complaint, as Northern Tea Merchants endeavour to produce a high quality product under hygienic conditions. I shall, therefore, investigate the cause of complaint and notify you as soon as I have some results.

I shall be grateful if you will quote number 07 on any future correspondence or contact with us

Yours sincerely

James Pogson

JAMES POGSON
DIRECTOR

NORTHERN TEA MERCHANTS LTD

Incorporating Classic Coffees.

Crown House
193 Chatsworth Road
Chesterfield
Derbyshire S40 2BA

Tel: (01246) 232600
Fax: (01246) 555991

Email: enquiries@northern-tea.com
Web: http://www.northern-tea.com

I apologise for the formality of this first letter
I will be more human in any subsequent letters!
I am waiting to be returned your tub of cocoa from
Finest China & will reply in full as soon as I have tested it.

Yours

With Compliments

NORTHERN TEA MERCHANTS

Incorporating Classic Coffees

Telephone: (01246) 232600 (Orders)
(01246) 233660 (Sales)
(01246) 233243 (Enquiries)
(01246) 278625 (Accounts)
Facsimile: (01246) 555991
E-mail: enquiries@northern-tea.com

TEA BAG MANUFACTURERS,
COFFEE ROASTERS,
PACKERS OF TEAS, COFFEES
AND VENDING PRODUCTS

Crown House
193 Chatsworth Road
Chesterfield
Derbyshire S40 2BA

WITHOUT PREJUDICE

RE: COMPLAINT 07

9th March 2010

Dear Mrs Stone

I am today in receipt of your cocoa powder, and I have tried it and made notes. It appears that your complaint is justified. The cocoa has above the normal amount of free fatty acids, hence the smell. This can be called rancidity. This very rarely occurs in alkalysed cocoa powder that has been correctly produced and handled. It has no physical difference in appearance to standard cocoa powder, and flows the same through an auger filler. In short, it is impossible to spot on a packing line. That is why it is important we use reputable suppliers who produce the cocoa powder in a safe and hygienic manner.

We take great steps to ensure we look after our cocoa powder whilst it is in stock here. We segregate it completely from other products and handle it in accordance with our independently audited quality manual. It is imported from one of the largest European processors of cocoa, Messrs Dutch Cocoa, via a reputable importer called HB Ingredients. I have also sent on the remainder of the cocoa to HB's Quality Assurance department for further analysis.

Yours is the only complaint we have received on this product from the packing run of 12 pallets (12096 drums) that we packed on 12th and 13th November 2009. Your tin was packed on the 12th and my packing records show nothing other than a problem-free packing run. I can only hope that we receive no more complaints and yours is an isolated one.

I have arranged from a packing run we are carrying out today for a case of 6 x 125g Food Thoughts Cocoa to be sent to you. I hope you will agree when you are trying it again that it is indeed an excellent quality Fairtrade product. I personally love the brownies and chocolate cake it makes. We actually use it for all the chocolate cakes we make in our café! (Please see our website on http://www.northern-tea.com/cafe.asp).

If I can be of any further service to you then please do not hesitate to contact me.

Yours sincerely

JAMES POGSON
DIRECTOR

Complaint Letter No. 15

Response: A lengthy telephone call from a very concerned health advisor at Philips Healthcare to investigate the problem with the bottle.

John Atwill
Managing Director (UK)
Philips Healthcare
Philips Centre
Philips Business Park
Guildford
Surrey GU2 8XH

Dear Mr Atwill

As a new mother and a user of Avent baby products, it is with great regret that I must put pen to paper.

I recently purchased a batch of Philips AVENT BPA free Airflex feeding bottles for my baby girl who was initially breast-feeding exclusively, but had to change to combination-feeding as she was not putting on enough weight.

This combination feeding has helped with my baby's weight but unfortunately she developed nipple confusion as the bottle teats are more fast-flowing than the breast. I am not blaming your product for causing this nipple confusion, but there is another issue with the teats that has given me cause to write.

Every time I go to bottle-feed my daughter, the teat shoots out milk squirting my baby in the face, which

- as you can imagine, is most upsetting for her. I wish this happened to be a one-off case, but unfortunately it occurs almost every feed without fail, and as a result – along with the nipple confusion, feeding has become a somewhat traumatic event.

I feel that a baby's first experiences with food have a profound effect on their eating habits for the rest of their life, and as the main supplier of baby feeding products, I believe this is something your company should investigate.

I look forward to hearing from you.

Yours sincerely
Ingrid Stone

Complaint Letter No. 16

By email to Queens Park Conservatives

```
Chris Philp
Queens Park Conservatives
1a Heath Hurst Road
London NW3 2RU

Dear Mr Philp

Thank you for your recent campaign
letter.

However, I am listed on the electoral
role as 'Ms' not 'Mrs', and I find it
somewhat old-fashioned (not to
mention presumptuous) that someone in
your admin department felt obliged to
alter my title.

As it happens, I am married but I
choose to use my maiden name with the
'Ms' for the reason that men do not
have their marital status mentioned
in their title, therefore why should
I?

I would expect this sort of
presumptuous grammar from an estate
agent's mail-out but not from a
political party trying to attract new
voters.

I look forward to hearing from you.

Yours sincerely
Ingrid Stone
```

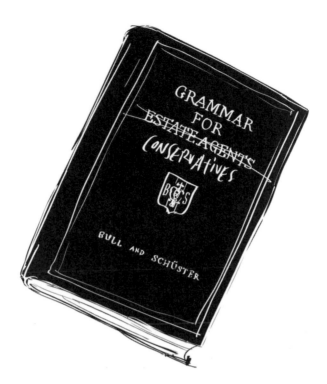

From: Chris Philp
To: "'Ingrid Stone'"
Subject: RE: Recent Campaign Letter

Dear Ms Stone,

I am very sorry for our mistake, the
database that we use is directly from
the electoral role, but sometimes
there are mistakes made.

I have changed your title on the
electoral register.

Sincere Apologies,
Chris Philp
Parliamentary Candidate for Hampstead
and Kilburn

Complaint Letter No. 17

Response: Replacement runners for chest of drawers sent directly from Sweden, although it must be said that IKEA appears to adopt a 'Scarlet Pimpernel' approach when dealing with its customers.

Mikael Ohlsson (President and CEO)
IKEA IT AB
Rönnowsg. 8
SE-251 08 Helsingborg
Skåne län
Sweden

Dear Mr Ohlsson

My husband and I recently bought your Hemnes three-drawer chest of drawers for our baby daughter's nursery. The drawers are a nice design but I must say that I am appalled by the shoddy quality of the build.

The drawers are none-too-simple to put together - and while I admire the Buddhist saying of life being a journey and not the destination, I do not appreciate this philosophy when it is applied to flat-pack furniture.

It was only as my husband and I had completed the chest of drawers when we discovered that two wheels from two different runners were split in half. Because of these errant wheels, two of the drawers refuse to open and close properly, which is most frustrating after spending a good couple of hours building the piece of furniture.

I have attached one of the faulty wheels that my husband found in the packaging, and I would be grateful if this matter could be resolved as soon as possible.

I look forward to hearing from you.

Yours sincerely
Ingrid Stone

From: Marilyn Cooper
To: Stone, Ingrid
Subject: IKEA

Dear Mrs Stone,

I am in receipt of a letter which was sent to IKEA @ Helsingborg dated 8th April.

Firstly please accept my apology for the delay in the IKEA UK response, any customer service correspondence received into IKEA Sweden is always re-directed, unanswered, back to the country of origin for action and response and unfortunately this can cause a delay to the ultimate resolution.

I was however very sorry to read that the item you purchased had broken parts included.

I realise that some of the IKEA items are not the easiest to complete and assemble and I sincerely apologise to you for this broken part error.

IKEA UK has a contact centre based in Rotherham and Peterborough 0845 355 2255 and all IKEA customer services co-workers are on hand to deal with any issue that an IKEA customer may be confronted with, a broken or missing part is actioned with immediate effect, whilst the customer is on the phone, an order is placed and those parts are sent direct to the customer via the IKEA parts department.

If the parts can be sent from an IKEA UK store parts department then this is actioned, if the item is a specific order then the request is submitted to IKEA globally parts department.

I have arranged for the parts to be sent to you and your case id is 6358797, the parts are ordered directly from IKEA Sweden who will ultimately send them direct to you or your home address, these should arrive with you shortly.

Thank you for your patience and for speed of any future resolution

that you may be faced with in
relation to any IKEA product it is
always best practice to firstly deal
with the IKEA contact centre customer
services or directly by re-visiting
the relevant IKEA store of purchase
who will action any issue for you.

I apologise to you again sincerely
for the delay in the resolution and
if you have already contacted or
re-visited an IKEA store and resolved
the issue directly please keep the
parts that have been ordered as a
spare.

Regards
Mrs Marilyn Cooper
IKEA UK and IE Customer Services
Specialist

From: Ingrid Stone
To: Marilyn Cooper
Subject: Fwd: IKEA

Dear Mrs Cooper

Thanks again for your help -

Just to let you know that I still
haven't received the parts from IKEA,
and the chest of drawers feels very
rickety indeed.

Please would you chase this up for
me?

Many thanks, and best regards
Ingrid

On 15 Jun, at 10:17, Marilyn Cooper wrote:

Dear Mrs Stone

I am assisting Mrs Cooper whilst she is on holiday leave.

I have now arranged to get the Wembley store to post out the fittings in which you should be in receipt of these within 3-5 days.

Please accept my apology on the delay.

Best regards

Julie Harrison
IKEA Customer Care

From: Ingrid Stone
To: Marilyn Cooper
Subject: Re: IKEA

Dear Marilyn / Julie

Many thanks for having the parts sent for the chest of drawers, but unfortunately they are the wrong parts.

The parts sent are the runners that fit on the drawers, but the parts we require (i.e. the damaged section) are the runners that are attached to the body of the chest.

Please can these be sent out to us.

Thanks again -

Best regards
Ingrid

On 22 Jun, at 09:14, Marilyn Cooper wrote:

Hi Ingrid,

I am so sorry about the confusion, it would appear that the parts you require come attached to the sides and are not packaged as a part so IKEA is unable to send this to you, if I could please request a contact telephone number IKEA will contact you and do an 'uplift and exchange' of the full item.

Hope the above assists you, the case id ICC15096119, if you can contact IKEA on 0845 355 1141 and quote the case id, customer services within IKEA Wembley will set it all up for you and arrange for the up and exchange to be arranged.

Please arrange for the item to be dismantled prior to collection,

Many thanks
Marilyn

From: Ingrid Stone
To: Marilyn Cooper
Subject: Re: IKEA

Thanks Marilyn, but unfortunately we can't dismantle the chest of drawers as it has been screwed together.

Please advise.

Best regards
Ingrid

From: Marilyn Cooper
To: Ingrid Stone
Subject: RE: IKEA

Hi Ingrid,

Thanks for the information but I am unable to assist you with a collection and uplift/exchange without the item being dismantled.

Would you be prepared to live with the item with a discount perhaps...?

I will assist you in any reasonable resolution but IKEA would definitely prefer you to dismantle and allow a complete full up and exchange to happen but this is your call so to speak now?

The offer is a gesture because the items you state are faulty are not a spare part so the only option available to IKEA to assist you is to up/exchange a dismantled item.

Just let me know your thoughts/requests and I will action,

Regards
Marilyn

Complaint Letter No. 18

Philip Rogerson
Chairman
Carillion Plc.
24 Birch Street
Wolverhampton
West Midlands WV1 4HY

Dear Mr Rogerson

If your company is so self-assured as to have vehicles carrying a sticker saying 'how's my driving?' then you must be prepared to experience the wrath of fellow motorists such as myself when the driving technique of your couriers is not quite up to scratch.

Driving along Victoria Road towards the A40 this morning, I found myself behind one of your drivers. There was very little traffic – and so there was no excuse for your courier to straddle both lanes as we approached the traffic lights. This is a particular pet hate of mine as it means the way is blocked for traffic to filter into the direction they require. Your driver seemed more intent on drawing on his cigarette than adhering to the Highway Code.

I look forward to hearing from you.

Yours sincerely
Ingrid Stone

From: Egginton Dawn   On Behalf Of
McDonough John
To: 'ingrid.stone@virgin.net
Subject: Complaint

Dear Ms. Stone,

Thank you for your letter dated 12th
May which Philip Rogerson, our
Chairman, has forwarded to me.

I can only apologise for any
inconvenience that you were caused on
your journey and I can assure you
that your comments have been noted.
Should you have a registration number
or any further details relating to
the vehicle in question, please let
me know and I will investigate the
matter further.

In the meantime, once again, please
accept my sincere apologies on behalf
of the Company.

Kind regards,
John McDonough
Chief Executive
Carillion Plc

Dawn Egginton | Carillion plc
PA to John McDonough, Chief Executive

Complaint Letter No. 19

Response: Eleven pounds to cover the cost of the Superfine Liner For Brows.

Janet Saunders
Clinique UK & Ireland General Manager
Clinique Laboratories LLC.
73-75 Grosvenor Street
London W1K 3BQ

Dear Ms Saunders

I have been wearing Clinique products almost as long as I have been wearing make-up, which I hasten to add is a fair amount of time. I love the products, and I am a contact-lens wearer so the hypoallergenic ingredients agree with me – in fact, most of the make-up I wear, along with my skincare is Clinique.

I was most upset when you stopped producing your Clinique Eyebrow Pencil With Brush, and hence I was forced to purchase the Superfine Liner For Brows. Your white-coated team insisted that this Superfine Liner was superior to its predecessor, but I beg to differ. The subsequent result is that this product is so unsubtle it gives the impression that the make-up wearer has had their eyebrows tattooed. In fact it makes me look as if I have applied the liner with a small child's felt tip pen – which is not a good look.

Another negative aspect to this liner is that there is no way of knowing how much of the liner is left. When I purchased it, I presumed it would have a transparent nib like your Quick Liner products and therefore know when the liner would be coming to the end of its little life. But it does not have this transparent casing, and therefore it is quite possible that one might find themselves caught short.

I am sorry to say that I will not be purchasing any more Superfine Liners For Brows, and in future I shall have to buy my eyebrow pencils from one of your competitors.

I am returning my Superfine Liner For Brows so that you can see this product's failings for yourself.

I look forward to hearing from you.

Yours sincerely
Ingrid Stone

Clinique Laboratories Limited
Constellation House 3 Kite's Croft Business Park Warsash Road Fareham Hants PO14 4FL
Telephone 0870 034 6700 Facsimile 0870 034 2700

Case reference No. 400500

Dear Ingrid,

We are in receipt of your letter dated 18 May 2010, enclosing Superfine Liner For Brows in shade Black/Brown.

While pleased you selected this product, we are sorry to learn of your disappointment with this product. As with all Clinique products, this product was extensively researched and tested prior to approval for manufacture. Some of the most important factors tested for are safety, aesthetic appeal, and efficacy. All product performance claims are substantiated at our Laboratories. Consumer response to this product has been positive, and we regret that you do not share in this opinion. Nevertheless, we recognise that skin types are highly individualised. Therefore, one of our other product formulations may produce the desired results. Since you are not satisfied, we are pleased to forward our cheque in the amount of £11.00 to refund your purchase price. We do hope that you will have the opportunity to discuss your experience with one of our counter representatives, who we are confident will be able to suggest a suitable replacement.

We trust that the above addresses your concern. We hope you will look to Clinique for all your skin care and beauty needs

Again, thank you for taking the time to share your thoughts and concerns.

Sincerely,

Tracy Cox
Consumer Care Centre
Global Consumer Communications

Registered No. 959265 England Registered Office 73 Grosvenor Street London W1K 3BQ

INVESTOR IN PEOPLE

Complaint Letter No. 20

Stuart Oetzmann
Managing Director
Metfield Bakery
23 Charles Wood Road
Rash's Green Industrial Estate
East Dereham NR19 1SX

Dear Mr Oetzmann

As regular consumers of your Organic Just Rye
Naturally Leavened Sourdough in your 'All Natural'
range, my husband and I were troubled to see that
you have ceased to use freshness-bags in which to
package the bread.

The freshness-bags meant that the bread was ripe for
eating for up to four or five days, whereas now it lasts
a miserly two before the bread grows stale. This is
most inconvenient. Not only that, it is a terrific
waste, as the loaf size is large and there is no way all
that bread can be eaten during such a short period of
time. One would have thought that with your
commitment to sustainable food, this would be of
some concern.

I look forward to hearing from you.

Yours sincerely
Ingrid Stone

From: "Stuart Oetzmann"
To: ingrid.stone@virgin.net
Subject: FW: Freshness Bags Delivery
Update

Dear Mrs Stone

Thank you for your letter of 15th
May.

We have had some difficulty with the
supply of these bags. At first we
were told the supplier wouldn't be
able to supply us as our order of
25000 bags was too small, despite
having supplied this size order into
All Natural for many years. We then
increased our order to 50000 for
which we have paid in advance and
were given a lead time of 10 weeks.

We had not been told of such a long
lead time at the time of purchase of
All Natural, and thus ran out of
bags. We had been given a date of
14th May for the delivery of our
order and have now been advised by
the manufacturer that our order will
now arrive at the beginning of June.
I am forwarding the email I have
received from the manufacturer to
you.

Please rest assured that we are
working very hard to resume use of
the freshness bags, and now that we
know of the lead times involved,
please also be assured that we will

strive to endeavour that we never run out again.

I hope that this email provides some reassurance to you. Many many thanks as well for purchasing our bread - I enclose our latest product list for you to see how our range has expanded this year.

Many thanks

Stuart Oetzmann
Director
The Metfield Bakery
23 Charleswood Road
East Dereham
Norfolk NR19 1SX

From: Manuela Peherstorfer
To: Stuart Oetzmann
Cc: Daniel Mettler
Subject: Freshness Bags Delivery Update

Hi Stuart,

Further to your phone call yesterday please note that the delivery date we provided was only an estimate. I am very sorry that I did not update you last week. At the moment we are aiming to deliver beginning of June due to a small delay.

I will let you know an exact date as
soon as we can confirm.

Many Thanks!

Kind Regards
Manuela Peherstorfer
Sales Office Manager
PAPIER-METTLER UK Ltd
Paper and Plastic Packaging
7 Parkway, Porters Wood,
St. Albans, AL3 6PA

Complaint Letter No. 21

John McCarthy
Chief Executive Officer
Poundland Ltd.
Wellmans Road
Willenhall
West Midlands WV13 2QT

Dear Mr McCarthy

I visited Poundland (Kilburn High Road branch) for my first time today in order to purchase a Funtastic Light Up Hairy Bug for my nine-month-old baby. My local baby centre has these toys and the babies go wild for them – so much so, that I decided to buy one for my little girl. I asked the woman running the play session at the centre where she obtained the light-up bugs from, and she mentioned Poundland.

It was interesting to see Poundland, especially after the publicity it has received recently, and there seemed to be quite a good range of products aimed at babies and children. In fact, not only did I purchase a Funtastic Light Up Hairy Bug, I also bought a Funtastic Light Up Panda ("Every Child's Favourite Friend!") I noticed on the label that the toys are designed for children of 36 months, yet seeing how widely available they are in my local baby centre, I decided that I would allow my baby to play with them but only under careful supervision. What I was unprepared for, however, was a sharp, seemingly broken shard of either glass or plastic within the rubber casing of the toy – like a piece of a broken light bulb, and it was lucky I spotted it before I allowed my baby to play with it.

I am quite appalled to have come across this – especially in a store that aims much of its merchandise towards children. This is not a question of a child being a minimum of 36 months; this is a case of damaged – and potentially dangerous products being on sale. I appreciate that your business is aimed at budget-minded consumers, but surely those consumers also deserve proper safety measures and quality control.

I have enclosed the Funtastic Light Up Hairy Bug (it might not have been so 'funtastic' having to deal with an injured infant), which as you can see, has barely been touched and still has its original label.

I look forward to hearing from you.

Yours sincerely
Ingrid Stone

Poundland®

Your Ref:

Our Ref: JMc/LM

Direct Line: 0121 526 8340

Fax: 0121 526 3090

Email: jim.mccarthy@poundland.co.uk

Dear Mrs Stone,

Thank you for your letter dated 21 July 2010 and please accept my apologies for the delay in responding. The letter was only received at head office on 29 July.

Due to the sensitivity of the product and it's ailment, I feel it best that I forward your letter to the Customer Relations team and the product to our Quality Assurance team for full investigation. You will receive a full reply in writing with our findings no later than 28 days from the date of this letter.

Please may I take this opportunity to apologise sincerely and I hope that you are able to continue shopping with us.

Yours sincerely
**For and on behalf of
POUNDLAND LIMITED**

**J McCarthy
Chief Executive**

Ps. We really do appreciate you bringing this serious matter to my attention and we will deal with it as a matter of significant urgency. My current understanding is that the product has been damaged or trodden on but returned to the display position. On Quality examination will determine if this is the case.

Poundland Limited, Wellmans Road
Willenhall, West Midlands WV13 2QT, UK

Telephone: +44 (0)121 568 7000
Fax: +44 (0)121 568 7007
www.poundland.com

Registered in England Company No: 2495645. Registered Office: Wellmans Road, Willenhall, West Midlands WV13 2QT

Complaint Letter No. 22

Response: A replacement Culinare Magi-Can can-opener.

Nick Cornwell
Managing Director
DKB Household UK Ltd.,
Bridge House
Eelmoor Road
Farnborough
Hampshire GU14 7UE

Dear Mr Cornwell

I bought the enclosed Culinare MagiCan can-opener
from Waitrose last week, as it looked like a good,
sturdy product.

The blades cut into the can well, but unfortunately
once the cutting has been completed, the can's plastic
'legs' refuse to open and it is impossible to remove the
can. It is especially annoying when trying to remove
a tin of tuna fish. I had this misfortune a couple of
days ago, and I quite literally had to force the plastic
legs of the can-opener apart. Of course the liquid in
which the tuna was contained went everywhere –
including over me, with everything smelling of fish,
which was most unpleasant.

Not only is the product entirely impractical, it is also
dangerous, as in trying to prise open the plastic legs
of the can-opener, the consumer's hand can slip and

cut themselves on the tin or the can-opener blades in the process.

In fact, with the Culinare MagiCan's reluctance to give over the can (rather like a dog refusing to let go of a stick), perhaps the product should be re-named a 'Can't-opener' or even a 'Shan't-opener'.

I look forward to hearing from you.

Yours sincerely
Ingrid Stone

DKB
DIETHELM KELLER BRANDS

DELIVERY NOTE   3490553

CONSUMER SALES/REPLACEMENTS
Bridge House
Eelmoor Road
Farnborough
Hampshire
GU14 7UE
United Kingdom

Delivery Address

DELIVERY NOTE
Date

Your reference
INGRID STONE
Order
Order Date

Invoice Address   251314

Page 1 / 1

Item-No. EAN-No. Cust.Prod.	Description	No of packs	Unit PackSize	Qty
C10000 5011268943263	MAGICAN WHITE	1	EA	1

We refer to our general terms of sale and delivery.

DATE DESPATCHED	: :	PROOF OF DELIVERY	: ....
TOTAL No OF CARTONS	:	SIGNED	: ....
TOTAL No OF PALLETS	:	FULL NAME	: ....
TOTAL No OF PALLET LIFTS	:	DATE	: ....
TOTAL WEIGHT	:	PALLETS EXCHANGED	: ....
BOOKING IN DATE	:	EXPORT COLLECTIONS	
TIME	:	COMPANY NAME	: ....
BOOKING REF	:	DRIVERS NAME	: ....
TRANSPORT REF	:	VEHICLE REGISTRATION	: ....
		DATE COLLECTED	: ....

DKB Household UK Limited
Bridge House
Eelmoor Road
Farnborough
Hampshire
GU14 7UE
GB United Kingdom

T +44 1252 522322
F +44 1252 522542

Reg. in England 1268346

BNP Paribas Fortis
5 Aldermanbury Square
London EC2V 7HR
VAT No. GB886266965
Swift Code GEBAGB22
Kto/Account 38244001
IBAN GB66GEBA40526238244001

Complaint Letter No. 23

Response: Situation remedied by Brent Council.

Councillor James Denselow
30 MOntrose Avenue
London NW6 6LB

Dear Mr Denselow

You would be mistaken if you thought both of the attached photographs were entries for the Turner Prize. In fact, only one of the photographs was ever an entry for the Turner Prize – the one of Tracey Emin's 'My Bed'. The other picture shows the state of the rubbish outside my home _after_ this morning's rubbish collection.

While it is admirable that your rubbish collection team have artistic aspirations, it is quite appalling they have left this amount of rubbish – in fact, they have created more mess than there was to start with. The Pampers box comes from my household, and which I originally put inside the bin. If you look at the photograph, you will see that it is now lying on the pavement, along with all manner of things – empty vodka bottles, cigarette packets – why not throw a used condom into the throng? You must surely be aware that rubbish attracts more rubbish, and if passers-by see litter carelessly strewn on the ground, it is often human nature to treat that area with the same lack of respect.

I am most concerned about this situation. It is – by no means, the first time that this has happened, and I am disgusted that this is what we are getting for our council tax. Not only that, as the parent of a small baby, I am deeply concerned that this area outside our building has become a breeding ground for germs.

Please would you investigate this matter as soon as possible.

Many thanks.

Yours sincerely
Ingrid Stone

From: James Denselow
To: ingrid.stone@virgin.net; Rope, Richard
Subject: Rubbish Collection – Winchester Avenue

Dear Richard,

Please see the email below from a constituent who has very just concerns with the quality of her rubbish collection.

Best,
Cllr. James Denselow

From: "Rope, Richard"
To: ingrid.stone@virgin.net
Subject: RE: Rubbish Collection -
Winchester Avenue

Ingrid,

Thank you for forwarding the picture.

The position with spillage is that
Veolia is required the clean up
spillage which is caused during the
bin emptying process. This photo does
not look like spillage as spillage is
usually found in the road where the
refuse cart stops.

Veolia is not required to take
flytipped items e.g. builders bags,
uncontained waste or clean up bin
areas that are open or "unsecure" as
in this case. Unfortunately, large
bins such as this are open to
everybody and attract fly tips as
well as people foraging in the bins
looking for food, or clothing or
other items.

Cleaning up bin sheds/areas is the
responsibility of the land owner, so
I suggest you contact them and look
at the possibility of them putting a
door, or gate up to protect the bin
area, or undertake regular cleaning
of area as part of their block
cleaning.

Hope the above that clarifies the
situation.

Regards
Richard

At 15:46, Ingrid Stone wrote:

Dear Richard

Thanks for your response, but if you look closely at the items around the bin, only one of the items is a fly-tipping object i.e. the Morans builders' bag. Everything else is regular garbage, including the Pampers box, which belonged to my household. The bins became this way immediately after the rubbish collection team departed. If this isn't clear, I would be happy to send you some more photographs that I took yesterday.

Therefore, I am sorry to say that this is their responsibility. Also, as already stated in my email to Cllr James Denselow, this is not the first time that this has happened.

Yours sincerely
Ingrid Stone

From: Ingrid Stone
Cc: Rope, Richard; Denselow, James
Subject: Re: Rubbish Collection - Winchester Avenue

Dear Richard

Following on from my email below, is there any update?

Many thanks, and best regards
Ingrid

From: "Rope, Richard"
To: ingrid.stone@virgin.net
Subject: RE: Rubbish Collection -
Winchester Avenue

Ingrid,

I have checked Winchester Ave and the
1100L bin at your property yesterday
and the collection had been done
properly.

Regards
Richard

Complaint Letter No. 24

Response: Six boxes of Dorset Cereals Simply Delicious Muesli.

> Peter Farquhar
> Chief Executive Officer
> Dorset Cereals Ltd
> Peverell Avenue East
> Poundbury
> Dorchester
> Dorset DT1 3WE
>
> Dear Mr Farquhar
>
> I have been an enthusiastic ingester of your Dorset Cereals Simply Delicious Muesli for around three years. It is an important part of my breakfast ritual, along with my freshly squeezed grapefruit juice and mug of green tea. In fact, in addition to the muesli and milk in my cereal bowl, I add a couple of teaspoons of yoghurt and a sliced banana. I am a woman who takes her breakfast seriously. I have a baby girl, and breakfast (which I eat along with a good book) is my little private time before my daughter wakes up.
>
> You can imagine my disappointment then, when it appears that your dried-fruit dispensing machine has been rationing the date content of late. According to your packaging, each box should contain 3.5% dates, which is half a percent less than the sunflower seeds and a whole percent more than the brazil nuts. I am no mathematician, but I do know that the date

content in my last few boxes of Dorset Cereals
Simply Delicious Muesli has amounted to naught. I
even find myself 'fishing' in the Tupperware
container (that holds my cereal) on a daily basis to
locate even a single piece of date.

This is most upsetting, particularly as Dorset Cereal's
strap-line is "honest, tasty and real". I certainly
agree with the 'tasty' and 'real', but in terms of
simple honesty, I feel that a few porkies have been
thrown in.

I look forward to hearing from you.

Yours sincerely
Ingrid Stone

dorset cereals®

Dear Ingrid

Thank you for your letter dated (no pun intended!) 23 November – and my apologies for taking so long to reply. Today is my first day in for a while, and your letter has been awaiting my return.

I am concerned and confused by your inability to find any dates in our Simply Delicious muesli. We certainly intend to put them into each pack at the stated 3.5%. I have even been down to the factory floor this afternoon and watched them going in to the mix! There can sometimes be a bit of variation between individual packs, but on the law of averages, if one pack has slightly fewer than 3.5%, then one of its mates will have a bit more.

Coincidentally, our Technical Manager is actually in Iran this week, checking out our date suppliers. We really do go that far to remain Honest, Tasty and Real.

Thank you for taking the trouble to write – I will arrange for some packs to be delivered to you. Hopefully, they will be date richer!

Yours

Peter Farquhar
Managing Director

Dorset Cereals Ltd, Peverell Avenue East,
Poundbury, Dorchester, Dorset DT1 3WE
T. +44 (0)1305 751 000 F. +44 (0)1305 751 020
www.dorsetcereals.co.uk pleasetellus@dorsetcereals.co.uk
Registered in England and Wales at the address as above. Registered No. 2867393

Complaint Letter No. 25

Response: Full kettle inspection and replacement.

David Maura
Chairman
Russell Hobbs, Inc.
3633 S. Flamingo Road
Miramar, Florida 33027
United States of America

Dear Mr Maura

It seems appalling that the very day the guarantee for my Montana kettle expires is the day that the kettle has quite literally run out of steam. I am certain this is not what Mr Russell and Mr Hobbs would have intended.

At first, I thought it might be a simple matter of it being a fuse, but then the kettle surprised me by switching on for one last, show-off breath. When the kettle refused to come on after that, I tweaked the cable and managed to get it to sneeze out its final sigh. But that was it, and now the kettle refuses to work.

Purchasing the Montana kettle was my first experience of buying a Russell Hobbs product, and I must say that having experienced such shoddy quality, I am reluctant to purchase anything from Russell Hobbs again.

I have enclosed the receipt (for the none-too-cheap price of £43.99), and seeing that I now need to purchase a new kettle, I would hope that your company will offer something in the way of compensation.

I look forward to hearing from you.

Yours sincerely
Ingrid Stone

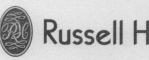
Russell Hobbs

Dear Ms Stone,

Thank you for your recent letter dated 12th December which has been forwarded for my attention as Managing Director for UK and Ireland.

The contents of your letter have been noted and I would first of all like to apologise for the problems that you have encountered with your Montana kettle just outside the guarantee period.

However, as I am sure you will appreciate, we will be unable to ascertain the precise cause of the fault on your kettle, or indeed rectify this, until we have been given an opportunity to inspect the product in our Service Department here in Manchester and I would therefore suggest that it be returned to us for full examination.

May I ask you to please pack the kettle carefully, enclosing a covering letter for reference purposes and send the parcel, clearly marked for the attention of Mr Andrew McKinlay, Technical Consumer Liaison & Investigations Technician to: - *Spectrum Brands (UK) Ltd, Customer Service Dept, Fir St, Failsworth, Manchester, M35 0HS.*

Please also be advised that the onus of posting is on the sender and I would recommend that proof of posting be obtained from your local Post Office.

Once your kettle has been received into out Customer Service Department it will be fully tested/inspected by Mr McKinlay and if its failure has been caused by a defect in manufacture or materials then the product will be replaced on a free of charge basis, as a gesture of goodwill.

Yours faithfully,

Tim Wright
Managing Director

Russell Hobbs Ltd., Fir Street, Failsworth, Manchester, M35 0HS, England.
Tel: +44 (0)161 947 3000 Fax: +44 (0)161 682 1708 email: postmaster@russellhobbs.com

Registered in England: 73700
A division of Russell Hobbs, Inc.

Complaint Letter No. 26

Response: Glue dots, glue tags and a range of products from Deva Designs latest collection.

Andrew Maddock
Managing Director
Deva Designs Ltd.
Chelford Close
Sealand Road Industrial Park
Chester CH1 4NE

Dear Mr Maddock

I purchased two rolls of Deva Designs wrapping paper (one silver, one gold) for my Christmas presents, and what should have been a fun gift-wrapping session turned out to be nothing less than a frustrating joke – and actually rather stressful.

The intermittent crackle I heard was not the crackle of logs on a fire, but rather the crackle of every single one of my Christmas presents that I had just wrapped, unwrapping themselves.

Appearances are deceptive, but your wrapping paper does not appear to have been designed for the purpose of wrapping presents. So keen is your wrapping paper to unwrap itself, that it has unwrapped itself before one can say 'Santa', let alone 'Christmas'. And in re-wrapping the presents, I had to use so much Sellotape – just to keep the wrapping paper on, that the gifts now look as if they have been wrapped in a straitjacket.

Having looked at your website, I see that you have collaborated with such reputable designers and companies as Designers Guild, and so I am surprised that your wrapping paper is so utterly ineffectual.

I look forward to hearing from you.

Yours sincerely
Ingrid Stone

———————————

From: "Andrew Maddock"
To: ingrid.stone@virgin.net
Subject: re letter dated 14th Dec

Dear Ingrid Stone,

thank you so much for you letter dated 14th December.

It is so important for us to get direct feedback from our customers and thank you for setting time a side to write to me.

I assume from your frustration of your presents 'unwrapping' themselves that you purchased 'heavy glitter' paper.

The heavy glitter paper looks stunning, but it can be a challenge to use.

The shop you purchased it from should of recommended either glue dots or glue tabs as they are designed to work with papers with special finishes.

I would also recommend that you finish the presents with a ribbon wrapped around
to keep everything secure and prevent any surprise openings!

I will send out to you today both glue dots and glue tabs to try.

I will also send to a range of our product from our latest collection as a thank you for your letter and I hope it will go some way to recompense you, for your 'wrapping frustrations'.

once again thank you for your letter and I do hope that you will continue to purchase Deva Designs gift wrap.

yours sincerely
Andrew Maddock

Managing Director
Deva Designs

Complaint Letter No. 27

Gordon Parsons
Senior Managing Director
Moto Holdings Ltd.
Toddington Service Area
Junction 11-12 M1 Southbound
Toddington
Bedfordshire LU5 6HR

Dear Mr Parsons

As I am sure you are familiar, there are many great spiritual sites in England's southwest – there is Stonehenge, sundown at Glastonbury Tor, among others. What I would never have expected is to come across relics in the baby-changing facilities at your Leigh Delamere Moto services, yet I feel I must add at this point, they were there for all the wrong reasons.

I visited your Leigh Delamere Moto services on Monday, 27th December with my husband and baby daughter. While I fully understand that we were travelling during the busy festive season – notwithstanding the dreadful queue for the ladies' that snaked from the toilets to the games area in the general concourse, nothing prepared me for the full horror of your baby-changing facilities.

Ironically, the first things I saw in the baby-change area were four separate bouquets of flowers – three still in their cellophane wrappings, one drooping in a vase. I shall never know if these flowers were the contributions of jilted husbands and wives who had been dumped somewhere between the M5 and the M4, or if the flowers were merely a memorial, a fond farewell to hygiene.

Even the cartoon monsters on the walls of the baby-change area looked concerned by the lack of cleanliness – the monster next to the nappy bin quite literally had his eyes popping out. The one toilet was blocked, and stuffed with paper and bodily fluids. This was rather alarming considering that the toilet is the perfect height for small children to dip their fingers into. And both the regular bin and the nappy bin were overflowing with rubbish. Someone had thoughtfully scattered the remains of their child's meal onto the floor – needless to say, it did not look exactly appetizing. But in terms of sheer bravado, nothing could compete with the filled nappy refuse sack that one of your visitors had carefully placed underneath one of the plastic armchairs, like an offering to the gods of ordure.

I am rather lost for words, especially seeing that Woman magazine has rated Moto services so highly – I can only think that your cleaners must have been put on high alert for that grand occasion. Or perhaps they were different cleaners – the same ones who, according to the many signs on the walls of the baby-change area, regularly check the facilities.

Following are a number of photographs to illustrate the issues in this letter. I hope you are concerned enough to investigate this matter as soon as possible.

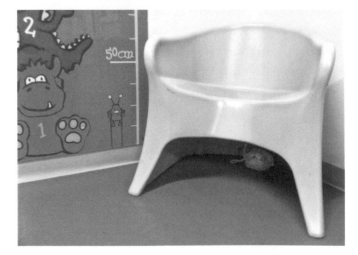

I look forward to hearing from you.

Yours sincerely
Ingrid Stone

TM/hke

Dear Mrs Stone

Thank you for your letter of 9 January, which has been passed to me by Gordon Parsons.

Please accept my sincere apologies for the terrible standards of hygiene experienced by you and your family during your recent visit to the baby changing facilities at our Leigh Delamere East service area. Please be assured that I am investigating this matter and will be in touch with you again shortly.

Once again, thank you for taking the time to bring this unfortunate matter to our attention.

Yours sincerely

TIM MOSS
CHIEF EXECUTIE OFFICER
MOTO HOSPITALITY LTD

Moto Hospitality Limited
PO Box 218, Toddington, Bedfordshire LU5 6QG   tel: +44 (0) 1525 873933   fax: +44 (0) 1525 878325   www.moto-way.com
Registered office: Moto Hospitality Ltd, Head Office, Toddington Service Area, Junction 12, M1 Motorway Southbound, Toddington, Bedfordshire, LU5 6HR. Registered no. 734299 England

Complaint Letter No. 28

Response: Sadly, no personal response from Sir Philip Green, but a nice telephone call from Arcadia's Customer Relations Department, along with a full refund.

Sir Philip Green
Arcadia Group Ltd.
Colegrave House
70 Berners Street
London W1T 3NL

Dear Sir Philip

I have been meaning to write to you for a while. I have been a loyal customer to Topshop for some fifteen years, and have always found the clothes to fit well and be on-trend and good value. That was until my mother bought me the enclosed trousers last Christmas.

The trousers were great for one-and-a-bit wearings. Feeling confident after the first wearing, I ventured out in them for a second occasion, only to discover that they were slipping down after the first hour of putting them on. With tiresome regularity, I spent an uncomfortable day having to hoist them up, and if I failed to do so, the crotch area of the trousers would end up at mid-thigh level so that they were more akin to a pair of old man's long-johns, which I am sure you will appreciate is not an especially good look. In fact, not only did this unintentional 'dropped' crotch provide a 'builder's bum' view, it proffered a full monty spectacle – as the fabric of the trousers is such, that one must either wear them with a thong, or no knickers at all.

As directed on the washing instructions, I took the trousers to be dry-cleaned, thinking that this might firm them up, but on a first wearing after collecting the trousers, the crotch simply dropped out of view.

This is most disappointing, as the trousers are a complete waste. As mentioned, they were a Christmas present from my mother, and I have been unable to wear them – plus I had to incur the expense and inconvenience of having the trousers dry-cleaned.

I would be grateful if you could look into this matter for me.

I look forward to hearing from you.

Yours sincerely
Ingrid Stone

Complaint Letter No. 29

N.B. The following letter was ghostwritten by the Dissatisfied Woman on behalf of a friend - hence the opening sentence: *"I am not normally driven to write letters of complaint"*.

Response: The full hammer price of £150 (all illustration fees, commission and loss warranty costs were reimbursed.)

Robert Brooks
Chairman
Bonhams & Brooks Ltd.
101 New Bond Street
London W1S 1SR

Dear Mr Brooks

I am not normally driven to write letters of complaint, however I feel compelled to put pen to paper following my last experience with Bonhams.

Subsequent to the death of my mother some fifteen months ago, my sister and I have had to dispose of much of my parents' estate. The quality furniture was auctioned at Bonhams, and spread over a number of months, it has totalled several thousand pounds. There are some remaining items to auction - including an Isfahan Persian carpet (valued at £6000 - £8000), a Shamshir sword (worth at least £2000) and an early Royal Doulton dinner service in mint condition. I have been in contact with Bonhams' staff regarding their sale.

Everything was fine until recently, when I submitted several small items for auction, and was offered settlement on three lots. The total hammer price on these lots was £150 - however, the cheque I received from Bonhams was for just £57.30. The £89.25 deduction for charges (plus VAT) comprised of £18.00 in illustration fees, £72 commission and £2.70 loss warranty.

It seems outrageous that Bonhams feels entitled to take nearly two-thirds of the hammer price and leave me with a sum that I could have got at a car boot sale. Indeed, the first of these three items sold was an Edwardian Elbow chair, which realised just £10! And from that £10, £30.18 was deducted by Bonhams leaving me with -£20.18 for the privilege of dealing with them. Surely the auctioneer would have known that; the chair should have remained unsold.

We had a good relationship with Michael Stevens, who helped us deal with a number of antiques at Pyes Hall, and I may have to seek his advice if I am not recompensed properly for these three (admittedly minor) lots. I am seriously considering withdrawing any future items from Bonhams as a matter of principle, and I am returning the cheque for £57.30, which - quite frankly, is an insult.

I would appreciate it if this matter is looked into as soon as possible.

Yours sincerely
Richard Courtauld

Bonhams [1793]

Bonhams
101 New Bond Street
London W1S 1SR

+44 (0) 20 7447 7447
+44 (0) 20 7447 7400 fax
www.bonhams.com

Dear Mr Courtauld

Thank you for your letter of 26th April. I am so sorry that your most recent experience with Bonhams was unsatisfactory. I quite understand that on the sale of your low value lots our minimum charges have added up to an excessive amount in this instance.

We have minimum charges in place because from a commercial point of view it is extremely difficult to handle profitably the sale of low value lots on a consistent basis.

Naturally I have no hesitation at all refunding in full all our charges for this most recent transaction as a gesture of goodwill. The original cheque which you returned has been cancelled and a replacement is also attached hereto.

Yours sincerely

Robert Brooks
Chairman

Bonhams 1793 Limited   London · New York · Paris · San Francisco · Los Angeles · Hong Kong · Melbourne · Dubai
Registered No 4326560   Registered Office: Montpelier Galleries Montpelier Street London SW7 1HH

Complaint Letter No. 30

Response: 4 x £1 Weetabix Ltd vouchers.

Ken Wood
Chief Executive Officer
Weetabix Ltd.
Burton Latimer
Kettering
Northants NN15 5JR

Dear Mr Wood

I usually buy a different brand of muesli, however my local shop only had Alpen (no added sugar) available.

As I tipped the cereal into my breakfast bowl, I could not help noticing that – even with my acute myopia, it bore no resemblance to the rather more voluptuous bowl of muesli in the photograph on the cereal box.

It goes without saying that when I added milk to the so-called Swiss recipe, the mixture settled into a sort of set mélange – more like something from a builders' merchants than the bowl of Alpine goodness it purports to be.

I must say that I am surprised Weetabix has not risen to the challenge when there is so much competition in the muesli market.

I look forward to hearing from you.

Yours sincerely
Ingrid Stone

Dear Ms Stone

Thank you for your letter of August 19th, though we were concerned to hear of your disappointing purchase of Alpen No Added Sugar.

I will make sure everyone in the factory and brand teams see your comments.

If you have retained the cereal and packaging could you please let me know. There will be a date and code on the top panel which will help me track the date and time of manufacture.

I look forward to hearing from you again soon.
Kind regards
Paul Blomley
Consumer Services Manager
The Weetabix Food Company

From: INGRID STONE
To: ConsumerService@Weetabix.Com
Subject: Re: Alpen enquiry 478308
Paul

Dear Paul

Many thanks for your email.

The date and code at the top of the
box is:

(Best Before) 21/07/2012
1202 19:34 B

Best regards
Ingrid

Sent from my iPhone

─────────────────────

From: "ConsumerService@Weetabix.Com"
To: "INGRID STONE"
Subject: Alpen enquiry 478308

Many thanks

I would be happy to send some
vouchers to put toward a future
purchase of any Weetabix product.

Please would you let me know if this
would be acceptable.

I have attached a product range
leaflet.

Kind regards
Paul

Complaint Letter No. 31

Response: Replacement products including fly-papers and a packet of window fly traps.

Edwin Allingham
Managing Director
STV International Ltd.
Forge House
Little Cressingham
Thetford IP25 6ND

Dear Mr Allingham

Due to a persistent *diptera* problem, my husband and I decided to purchase your Zero In Fly Bell Insect Catcher.

Despite the fly bell's somewhat Heath Robinson appearance, we understood your company to be a leader in the pest control market, and therefore we were optimistic.

The product certainly attracted the fly (as it said it would on the back of the packet), but perhaps the fly was merely curious by its extraordinary appearance. However, while the Zero In Fly Bell Insect Catcher's seduction technique is undoubtable, its trapping ability is completely useless – in that once the fly was done with its sticky seductress, the fly had no problem whatsoever in departing from the adhesive landing strip.

On a rather more frivolous note, I do like the names you have chosen for your various products – for example, 'The Big Cheese' mouse trap is great. How about renaming the Zero In Fly Bell Insect Catcher 'A-Catcher-in The Fly' (with apologies to JD Salinger)?

In the meantime, I would be most grateful if you would investigate the above matter (I have enclosed the unused fly bells). At present, your Zero In Fly Bell Insect Catcher is completely ineffective, but well-named (it catches Zero In it) – and a wasted purchase. The fly continues to walk free.

I look forward to hearing from you.

Yours sincerely
Ingrid Stone

INTERNATIONAL LTD

Forge House, Little Cressingham,
Thetford, Norfolk IP25 6ND.
Tel: +44 (0)1953 881580   Fax: +44 (0)1953 881452
Email: info@stvpestcontrol.com
www.stvpestcontrol.com

Reference: RAW068

Dear Ingrid

Thank you for your letter dated the 12th December. I was very sorry to read of the problems you had with the Zeroin 'Fly Bell' i can assure you this is not something that happens a lot so it may be how they were stored in the shop. I did pass you letter onto Edwin and he has seen your comments.

As the Fly bells did not work for you please accept some replacement products to try. I have sent you some replacement Fly papers which i think you will find satisfactory. I have also sent you a pack of 'Window fly traps' for you to try.

Once again we are very sorry the Fly bells did not work for you i can assure you it is very rare for us to get a complaint on this product. I have sent you a catalogue so you can view all our products.

If i can be of further assistance please don't hesitate to contact me on 01953 881580 where i will e happy to help. Alternatively please contact me on my email address which is supplied below.

Thank you

Kind Regards

Rebecca Waterfall
ST V Customer Service Team Leader
Tel: 01953 881580
rwaterfall@stvpestcontrol.com

Complaint Letter No. 32

Response: £5 off voucher against purchases for Always, Alldays and Tampax (valid for 3 months).

Irwin Lee
General Manager UK & Ireland
Procter & Gamble UK
The Heights
Brooklands
Weybridge
Surrey KT13 0XP

Dear Mr Lee

First of all, seasons greetings to you and your team at Proctor & Gamble UK. Wishing you a very happy new year.

I hate to reveal my intimate habits so early on in a letter, but I recently purchased a box of Tampax Compak® tampons, as Lil-lets - which I normally use each month, were not available at my local shop.

Like Lil-lets, the Tampax Compak® promises to be small and discreet, yet yours offers all manner of wonders, including a V Opening™ (whatever that might be – unless of course it is referring to the consumer's 'V' opening) a Protective Skirt™ and a Compak® retractable applicator. But while these technical advances might look impressive on the back of a cardboard box, they are completely meaningless when they fail to do the job. In fact, the Compak®

retractable applicator refused to expel its tampon (in much the same way as a parachute refusing to open), and I ended up having to prise out the white rayon mouse and manually position it. And it wasn't just the one. Over the course of two days, I did it five times (so to speak), and each Tampax Compak® declined to reveal itself, hiding itself within the confines of its Protective Skirt™.

I would go so far - if you will excuse the pun, to call this a duff product. Not only that, the Protective Skirt™, applicator and sweet-packet-style outer packaging are a waste of the earth's resources.

I have enclosed the remaining tampons in its original box, and look forward to hearing from you.

Yours sincerely
Ingrid Stone

Our ref: 10630415

Dear Ms. Stone,

Further to our previous correspondence, I'm pleased to inform you that the product you returned to us has been found to meet our quality specifications.

We have stringent quality checks in place at our factory designed to ensure that our products are made correctly. Please see below analysis of the Tampax:

Three Compak Super tampons arrived in closed wrappers for investigation.
Actions
Checked all quality and line documentation including finished product release documentations.
Samples sent to lab to do attribute check and measure expulsion force.
Conclusions
Budapest plant received three Compak Super tampons in closed wrappers for investigation. Received samples look like normal, they didn't have any quality deviation. Received tampons expulsion force tests and lengths are within specification.
All quality documentations for the given day of production were checked. There was no defect found on the line on this production day. The Daily History Records were also checked. There were no line stops that could cause this problem. The quality sampling procedure was properly followed (required tampons every 30 minutes and 1 carton every hour for wrapper, tampon and applicator quality) and all requirements were met. The stop and reject reports were also checked and on both cells the systems worked well.
We didn't see any functionality deviation and there were no action taken on the cells that could affect this type of problem.
Based on the investigation we could not define actions regarding this complaint.
Data will be monitored to establish if trends exist which may require further action.

In the hope that you will return to using our product with confidence, I have attached a voucher (valid for 3 months) which can be put toward a future purchase.

Thank you for allowing us to look into this matter for you.

Yours sincerely,

Complaint Letter No. 33

Response: 2 x boxes Jelly Belly 10 Individual Flavours, 2 x boxes Jelly Belly Fruit Bowl, 2 x packets Jelly Belly Fruit Bowl, 2 x Jelly Belly fridge magnets.

Tony Alfano
Managing Director
Best Imports Ltd.
Best House, Units 4 & 5 Alban Park
Hatfield Road
St Albans
Herts L4 0JJ

Dear Mr Alfano

Wishing you a happy new year, I hope it turns out to be a good one.

I am sorry to be a killjoy at the start of the year, but I thought it important you know about my neighbour's recent experience with Kirkland Signature Jelly Belly Gourmet Jelly Beans.

Having a family with a sweet tooth, my neighbour purchased the tub of jelly beans from Costco in time for the festive season. As I am sure you are aware, a big part of Jelly Belly's appeal is the fun to be had in recreating the recipes suggested in the enclosed Menu And Recipe Guide. However, three of the four recipes have raspberry beans as part of the ingredients ('Berry Smoothie', 'Poached Pear in Raspberry Sauce' and 'Fruit Salad'), and there were no raspberry-flavoured beans in the jar at all.

To be honest, I am not entirely sure who is responsible for this oversight, as there are several company names involved with this one product. There is Costco, Costco's Kirkland brand and Jelly Belly - and of course, Best Imports Ltd. is a separate business importing Jelly Belly jelly beans. But rather than embark on a chicken-and-egg detective mission, I thought you might be able to help seeing as your company is responsible for Jelly Belly in the UK. For your reference, the item number of the product is 730755.

Just because the tub of jelly beans was sold as part of Costco's Kirkland brand should be no excuse for sloppiness. Costco consumers are equally as important as those who might shop at a more exclusive store, and it is dreadful that Costco customers should have to draw the short straw when it comes to seemingly biased packaging. Indeed, why should they have to put up with an inferior product?

I look forward to hearing from you.

Yours sincerely
Ingrid Stone

From: "Mallea, Ana"
To: "ingrid.stone@virgin.net"
Cc: "Foster, Charles" "Annie
Metlikovec - Best Imports (UK)" Tony
Alfano - Best Imports UK, Victoria
Reeves - Best Imports
Subject: Jelly Belly Kirkland
Signature - 45 Assorted Flavors

Dear Ms. Stone,

Thank you for your letter to Best
Imports, Ltd.

While Best Imports is Jelly Belly's
authorized distributor for the UK,
the product we market & sell through
Costco International is independent
of Best Imports.

Thank you for bringing this point to
our attention, and rest assured we
are taking the necessary corrective
action. In appreciation of your
neighbor's support, as well as yours,
I will coordinate a sample order of
Jelly Belly product through Best
Imports and send it to the address
provided.

Do not hesitate to contact me with
further questions or concerns.
Regards. Ana
JELLY BELLY CANDY COMPANY
Confectioners of Excellence Since
1898

ANA MALLEA
INTERNATIONAL BUSINESS MANAGER
ONE JELLY BELLY LANE ● FAIRFIELD, CA
94533-6741 U.S.A.
TEL (707) 399-2765 ● FAX (707) 399-
2363

BEST IMPORTS
The world's finest confectionery

Dear Ms Stone

RE: Kirkland Signature Bean Jar

Please find enclosed some complementary Jelly Belly ® jelly bean products that we have been requested to deliver to you by the US manufacturer who I believe has been in direct contact regarding the Kirkland Costco Jelly Belly jar labelling.

Perhaps you would be kind enough to share them with your neighbour.
We hope you both enjoy them.

Sweet Regards

A.Metlikovec
Customer Services

encl.

BEST IMPORTS LTD, BEST HOUSE, UNITS 4 & 5 ALBAN PARK, HATFIELD ROAD, ST ALBANS, HERTFORDSHIRE AL4 0JJ
TEL 01727 829 010   FAX 01727 829 011   Email: info@bestimports.co.uk
www.bestimports.co.uk   www.jellybelly-uk.com   www.whatsyourfavouriteflavour.co.uk   www.sportbeans.co.uk

VAT No: 381 8068 34

Complaint Letter No. 34

Response: A replacement butter dish.

Nick Ryder
Managing Director
Le Creuset (UK) Ltd.
Le Creuset House
83 Livingstone Road
Andover
Hampshire SP10 5QZ

Dear Mr Ryder

I hope you had a good festive season.

I have loved the Le Creuset brand for as long as I can
remember. My parents were given a selection of blue
Le Creuset pans and casserole dishes on their wedding
day (which was sadly divided up between the two of
them when they divorced – although it must be said
that the pans were in no way responsible for my
mother and father's marital problems), and over the
years I have slowly been building my own collection.

My last purchase was a white Le Creuset butter dish.
I was attracted to its fine retro styling, and I liked
the quirky, yet entirely practical thing of being able
to warm butter in its dish section in the oven.
However, unlike your other products – which are
beautifully made, the butter dish's handle came away
in my hands as I lifted its lid a couple of days ago.

It was just as well that the butter dish was at room temperature. Had the dish been warm with hot butter, it might have been a very painful experience.

This is most disappointing - and entirely unexpected as I have never had a problem with Le Creuset products before, but unfortunately I find myself having to enclose a faulty butter lid.

I look forward to hearing from you.

Yours sincerely
Ingrid Stone

Transcript of a telephone message from a very nice-sounding woman called Laura.

Good afternoon, this is a message for Ingrid Stone. My name's Laura. I'm calling from Le Creuset about the butter dish lid you've returned to us. This is just a call to let you know we have received that. It has been inspected and we can verify there was a fault with the handle. It shouldn't have broken in the way that it has done, so you've been very unlucky there. So we're going to order a replacement for you today and a new butter dish with lid and base. We say fourteen days for delivery but I suspect that it will be with you sooner. If you have any questions or queries the free helpline number is 0800 373792. Many thanks.

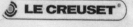

Delivery Note

Le Creuset L
Le Creuset Ho
Walworth Busine
Andover
Hampshire SP10 5C

Phone No.   0126-
Fax No.   01264 3

Sell-to Customer No.   C000003

Customer Ref. No.   INGRID STONE 100112

Shipment No.   SS053974
Shipment Date
Order No.   SO040821
WHS No.   WSH048820

No.	Description	EDI Item Ref.	Quantity	Unit of Measure
9101580068	Butter Dish Almd		1	Each

Bill-to Address
Customer Replacements
Andover
HAMPSHIRE SP103RU
United Kingdom

FREE OF CHARGE REPLACEMENT

TO BE POSTED - HOLD BALANCES

Complaint Letter No. 35

Response: £10.00 worth of postal orders.

Jim Moseley
Managing Director UK, Ireland & Nordic Markets
General Mills UK Limited
1 George Street
Uxbridge, Middlesex UB8 1QQ

Dear Mr Moseley

Let me begin this letter by saying that Jus-Rol is
marvelous. Jus-Rol Janet has saved my culinary
skin more than once, but I am afraid that she must
have been out partying with the best on New Years
Eve as your Jus-Rol vol-au-vent pastry cases failed to
rise to the occasion.

Quite honestly, I do not know what happened. I
spaced the cases evenly on a baking tray and brushed
the rims with milk, yet the mushroom and celeriac
vol-au-vents (which I had created for an eighties-
themed New Years Eve birthday party) barely made it
past the rather more lowly height of a potato waffle.

It might have had something to do with the lids. Or
the lack of appropriate instructions. There was no
mention of lids on the "how to cook" side of the box, or
indeed what to do with them. To make up for this
deficiency, I found myself having to tease out all 36
of the lids (which were pitifully thin) from the case
bottoms with a knife, which I have to say was

incredibly fiddly, and certainly unexpected coming from a ready-made convenience product like Jus-Rol. And when I finally positioned these lids onto the main 'body' of the vol-au-vent cases (surgical training might have helped - or at the very least, a pair of tweezers), they all but sank into the mushroom and celeriac filling.

Sadly, I found this to be an exceedingly ineffective and confusing product, and it is certainly something you should investigate. The "how to cook" instructions need to be looked at for starters (so to speak).

I look forward to hearing from you.

Yours sincerely
Ingrid Stone

Dear Stone

We would like to thank you for contacting us regarding your dissatisfaction with a recent purchase of our Jus-Rol Vol-auVent product.

We consider it of paramount importance that every customer is satisfied with our products and are very grateful that this matter has been brought to our attention.

After receiving your letter, we notified our Manufacturing and Quality Assurance staff of your complaint and after investigating this matter they have now provided us with a response.

Your letter mentioned that our vol au vents had some kind of 'lids' on them which were very difficult to remove. In reality, what you described as lids should have been removed by the appropriate machinery that cuts them. This product has no lid thus the packaging offered no instructions, as you rightly mentioned, regarding this. The tops of the vol au vents should have been cut and removed and should have also been inspected by personnel at the manufacturing line before they were packaged. On this occasion, it is clear that this error managed to leave our facility undetected and we are truly sorry for this as it meant that you had to spend more time in preparation of your mushroom and celeriac vol au vents.

Food quality and safety at Jus-Rol are our prime concerns and considerable care is taken in the preparation and packaging of our products. We take every practicable precaution to ensure that our products reach our customers in excellent condition.

Once again, we would like to apologise for any inconvenience that you have experienced and would like to restore your confidence in our products. Please accept the enclosed complimentary postal orders as a gesture of goodwill.

We hope you will continue to use and enjoy our Jus-Rol products.

Yours sincerely,

A. Bristow

A. Bristow
Consumer Relations

Ref: 2012/01/19-1123GB

Jus-Rol, PO Box 363, Uxbridge, Middlesex, UB8 1YT.
Frozen Products Tel: UK 0800 125 577 Ireland 1800 535 115,
Chilled Prodcuts Tel: UK 0800 028 0089 Ireland 1800 535 115
General Mills UK – Registered Office: Harman House, 1 George Street, Uxbridge UB8 1QQ
Incorporated in England and Wales. Company No. 4633664

Complaint Letter No. 36

Response: A replacement 'Stonehenge' cedar wood, bergamot and amber candle, plus an additional candle from Archipelago's 'Black Forest' range.

David Klass
President
Archipelago Botanicals
1834 East 22nd Street
Los Angeles
CA 90058
USA

Dear Mr Klass

I was bought one of your beautiful Stonehenge Glass Jar candles for my birthday by a friend of mine, who is a woman of great taste. Positioned on my coffee table (along with my agate coasters and stack of coffee table books), the candle looked wonderful and smelt even better. I adore cedar wood - and yours fares very well indeed, and my friend had gone out of her way to get me a candle with that particular scent.

Sadly that pleasure did not last. After around four burnings, the wick was nowhere to be seen (indeed I had the same problem after each initial burning), and out of sheer frustration, I found myself embarking on a full-scale digging expedition to locate the lost wick. Indiana Jones would have returned as empty-handed as I did from such a trip.

I have attached a couple of photographs to illustrate the current state of the candle. As you can see, it is entirely unsatisfactory; the Stonehenge is a mess. Unfortunately, the candle is quite heavy, and therefore impractical to return to your address in California, but I have retained it should you wish me to send it on.

I look forward to hearing from you.

Yours sincerely
Ingrid Stone

Dear Ingrid
Further to David Klass's letter, I was sorry to hear of your experience with the Stonehenge candle.
It doesn't mitigate your inconvenience but this is a very rare occurrence. So hopefully, the replacement we are enclosing will burn well. As an extra token, I am enclosing an extra candle from a similar fragrance family — Black Forest — for you to enjoy. Jerry Adler
Best regards

WITH COMPLIMENTS

a m
A D L E R
MARKETING

Adler Marketing Ltd.,
The Rear Barn, Manor Farm,
124 Manor Road North,
Thames Ditton KT7 0BH

Tel: +44 (0)20 8398 9744
Fax: +44 (0)20 8398 9731

From: David Klass
To: "ingrid.stone@virgin.net"
Subject: Archipelago / Stonehenge Jar
Candle

Dear Ingrid,

I just received your letter and
pictures describing the problem with
our Stonehenge Candle.

First, I am so sorry to hear that you
had a problem with one of our
products – and so appreciative that
you actually took the time to report
it. Our candles normally burn
wonderfully, and this particular
candle happens to be one of my
personal favorites.

If you still have the candle, can you
email the little lot code that
appears on the bottom label? With
that lot code information, I can
arrange to get the retained samples
from that particular batch back into
the lab for testing.

Without the benefit of that lot code
and the additional testing that will
follow, it's difficult for me to
determine exactly what went wrong.
If I had to guess, I would say:

- It could be the natural oils used in
  that batch are causing the candle to
  self-extinguish; however, we test
  all raw materials for burning issues
  upon receipt, and we haven't
  received any similar reports on this
  blend.

- It could also be that the wick was trimmed too short – either before you got it, or after you started using it. A wick that is too short can cause the flame to "drown" in the wax pool – resulting in the types of problems you are reporting.
- It could also be the result of burning the candle for too little of time. (I don't know if this is the case, but we have gotten reports in the past where people light the candle, burn it for a few minutes, and then quickly extinguish it in an attempt to lengthen its useful life. (The problem is that the wick starts to tunnel down into the wax, ultimately creating a situation where the flame can no longer get enough oxygen to burn properly)).

In the meantime, I am going to ask our Agent in London to send you a replacement.

I hope that you are able to provide the lot code, and that this unfortunate experience does not cause you to be reluctant to try our products in the future.

Again, thank you for letting us know.

Sincerely,

David Klass
President
Archipelago, Inc.
1834 East Twenty Second Street
Los Angeles, CA 90058

Complaint Letter No. 37

Response: £35 Tesco Moneycard.

Phillip Clarke
Group Chief Executive
Tesco PLC
New Tesco House
Delamare Road
Cheshunt
Herts EN8 9SL

Dear Mr Clarke

I recently purchased a 25-pack of your Tesco Party! pearlised balloons. The colours are lovely and they were absolutely perfect for the Bollywood-themed party I put on in a friend's garden.

That delight, however, was short-lived. Five out of the 25 pack of balloons exploded (enclosed) which was most upsetting for the children present. One of the infants was crying.

I trust your Tesco own-brand condoms are more reliable (let's hope they are of the Tesco Extra ilk rather than "Every little helps"). As it is, your balloons were something of a let down.

I look forward to hearing from you.

Yours sincerely
Ingrid Stone

TESCO PLC

TESCO HOUSE, DELAMARE ROAD, CHESHUNT, HERTS. EN8 9SL
Telephone: 01992 632222

Our Ref: 13792856

Dear Ms Stone

Thank you for your letter addressed to Philip Clarke, to which I have been asked to respond. Please accept my sincere apologies for the delay in my reply.

I was very sorry to learn of your disappointment with the Tesco 25 Assorted Pearl balloons you purchased and I regret any upset which was caused when five balloons exploded as you were organising a party.

The samples you kindly returned have now been analysed by our Technical Manager for this product range. She was equally sorry to learn of the problem and has discussed the matter with our supplier. Please be assured all necessary manufacturing controls will be increased to prevent a similar situation happening again.

It is always disappointing when a customer has cause to complain about any of the products we sell and, as a gesture of goodwill for any upset which has been caused, I have enclosed a £35.00 Tesco Moneycard with my apologies and best wishes.

Thank you for bringing this matter to the attention of the Chief Executive. Once again please accept my apologies for the delay in my response and any upset caused.

Yours sincerely

Hickling

Frances Hickling
Chief Executive's Office

Directors:
Sir Richard Broadbent (Chairman), P.A. Clarke (Chief Executive), G.R. Bullock, P.J. Cescau (Senior Independent Director), S.J. Chambers, K.R. Cook, K.G. Hanna, K.J. Hydon, T.J.R. Mason, L. McIlwee, Dame Lucy Neville-Rolfe DBE, CMG, FCIS, D. Oppenheimer, J.A. Tammenoms Bakker.

J.M. Lloyd (Company Secretary)

Registered in England and Wales: No. 445790. Registered office: Tesco House, Delamare Road, Cheshunt, Herts. EN8 9SL   VAT Registration Number: GB 220 4302 31

Complaint Letter No. 38

No response.

Chairman & CEO
Universal Music Group UK Ltd.
364-366 Kensington High Street
London W14 8NS

Dear Mr Hole

First of all, I would like to congratulate you on your
new role at Universal Music Group International.

I am sorry to mar your first month, but I was
compelled to write after discovering a typo on my The
Very Best of Michael Nyman: Film Music 1980-2001
CD (please see photograph below) that I purchased last
month.

I appreciate that the CD was produced by Virgin Records, but my understanding is that Virgin Records is now owned by Universal Music Group International.

The music sounds like Michael Nyman all right, but how am I to be sure it is not by someone called Micheal Nyman posing as Mr Nyman himself? Or perhaps it is like those fake designer handbags so lovingly copied, except for one small slip-up. I note that the CD cover has the correct spelling.

I should think the real Michael Nyman would be appalled if he knew of this error.

I look forward to hearing from you.

Yours sincerely
Ingrid Stone

A Satisfied Woman

To those who made the extra effort to apologise, who took the time to investigate one date less in a box of muesli - to the unsung heroes listed below, this oft-dissatisfied woman applauds you.

Sir Richard Branson – Virgin Management Ltd.
Ron Cox – Corus Hotel, Hyde Park
Ian Dallow – Debenhams Plc.
Sir Michael Rake – BT Group Plc.
Willie Walsh – British Airways Plc.
Steve Jobs – Apple Inc.
James Pogson – Product Chain Ltd.
Peter Farquhar – Dorset Cereals Ltd.
Andrew Maddock – Deva Designs Ltd.
Robert Brooks – Bonhams & Brooks Ltd.
Tony Alfano – Best Imports Ltd.
David Klass – Archipelago Botanicals
Philip Clarke – Tesco Plc.

Further Browsing

Letters Of A Dissatisfied Woman
www.lettersofadissatisfiedwoman.com

Watchdog
www.bbc.co.uk/watchdog
"My mission statement is to have all customers treated like royalty. Any chairman of a public company providing less-than-perfect service needs to fasten his or her seat belt and adopt the brace position."

-Anne Robinson

Mary Portas
www.maryportas.com
O Mary, you are marvellous. I have a bit of a crush on you.

Money Saving Expert
www.moneysavingexpert.com

The very dashing Martin Lewis gives us the lowdown on how to make the most of our money.

Savvy Woman
www.savvywoman.co.uk
The Pennells is mightier than the sword. Sarah Pennells' jargon-busting guide to saving for the life you want.

Which?
www.which.co.uk
Power to the people, Which? makes good consumer sense.

Acknowledgments

To my father Irving Stone and Grandpa Tony who trained me up in the dark arts of writing a good letter – and my mother Valerie Blumenthal for always encouraging me and being an inspiration.

To Tim Rockins for his beautiful artwork and for being so spot-on in interpreting my ideas.

A heartfelt Thank You to the following people for their support, help and enthusiasm for the project:

Geoff Fisher, Sophie Sweatman, Celine Castclino, Kate Monro, Margaret Rodgers, Emily Hall, Beth Hale, Oliver Parker, Rosanna Gardner, Leonora Merry and Will Green.

About The Author

Ingrid Stone is a full-time writer and copywriter having worked in television for nine years, along with a short stint in the film industry and as a performer on stage and the radio. She has written a novel A KNIFE AND A FORK and a children's book in addition to LETTERS OF A DISSATISFIED WOMAN, which is based on her popular blog www.lettersofadissatisfiedwoman.com

About The Illustrator

Tim Rockins played a pivotal role in all visual aspects of the multi-platinum cartoon pop band Gorillaz while working with Jamie Hewlett at Zombie Flesh Eaters. He has created artwork for Kate Moss, Damon Albarn, Yoko Ono, Primal Scream, Frost French, Lily Allen, Jake Chapman, Terry de Havilland, Agent Provocateur, Luella Bartley and many others. To see more of his work, his website is www.timrockins.com